CLEAN TIME

CLEAN TIME

Short Stories and First-hand Accounts of Addiction

Northern Bridge Productions

First published in Great Britain in 2004 by
Northern Bridge Productions
Flat 7, 2 Albert Terrace
London NW1 7SU
email: addiction@amberbridge.co.uk
www.amberbridge.co.uk

© 2004 by Northern Bridge Productions

ISBN 0-9549301-0-X

Typeset by Ray Davues
Printed in Great Britain by
Biddles Ltd, King's Lynn, Norfolk

Contents

Preface

I have sometimes wondered whether the fruit in the garden of Eden was in a state of fermentation when Eve gave it to Adam; whether the devil introduced certain substances at the very beginning in order to deceive and confuse mankind with the promise of instant, spurious bliss. So that now the heavy drinker, the occasional user may be aware that the pleasurable effects fade, leaving depression in their wake but the alcoholic, the addict cling to the vain belief that they can recapture that prelapsarian joy, not realising that the opportunity of joy precedes the satanic substance and is destroyed by it. The substance is a snare and a delusion. Addiction can be seen as a misguided quest in pursuit of the spiritual and it may be that to understand this is to start on the road to recovery and wholeness.

Alice Thomas Ellis

Foreword

Northern Bridge Productions, a charitable Trust, set up in November 1999, uses drama and psycho-drama therapy to alleviate the suffering of people who are, or fear they are, addicted. We also help their families and partners and raise awareness of the nature and consequences of addiction. We believe addiction has become an overwhelming problem and few families and workplaces are not affected to some degree by its influence and result.

Our project is divided into two parts. The performance by actors of commissioned scripts by professional writers, followed by audience discussion in theatres and venues across the UK and, secondly, a series of affordable workshops facilitated by highly qualified therapists.

The purpose of the workshop is to challenge addiction by using the addict's untapped creativity, to accept and come to terms with and then replace substance craving. We believe there is a vital opportunity at the very moment of craving and the addict reaching out for the substance is potentially the most alive and creative moment. Using expressional work designed to reroute the craving into a creative experience can block the use of substances and buy time. Craving and creativity share the same route process.

Professional actors and then the workshop members play the family member, addict and the substance itself, its nature defined by each of the participants. The substance is no longer seen as a simple bottle, a line of powder, but in its deeper reality as destroyer, rival, false lover, necessary shield. Both theatre performances and the workshops give an opportunity to explore the addict's world, the dilemma of partners and family, the process of finding solutions.

We are an expanding group made up from all fields of life dissatisfied with the existing 'treatment' of addiction and we want to find solutions to seemingly unresolvable conditions. We believe that addiction does not belong in any area, medical, religious, sociological. It is life drama.

What is addiction? The medical profession cannot agree. The addicts themselves don't know. Is it genetic? Behavioural? Is it an emotional flaw caused during the earliest stage of life by insufficient feeding and holding? Is it an allergy? A disease? Does it result from low self-esteem? Where does the heavy user cross the line and become the suffering addict?

The sensation is described as 'the emptiness inside', the 'inner void' which produces a need which, in turn, becomes the unbearable craving. The substance of choice: alcohol, cocaine, food, seems to be the solution. Behind the chemically induced bravado the collapsed person feels worthless, lonely, alienated from others. Active addiction is an attempt to put something between the worthless self and the scary world.

Professional scripts create a safe way in which to unpeel the layers of denial and find solutions. These written texts are effective in allowing people to open up and express painful feelings, and we have found that this self-expression leads to increased self-esteem, awareness and change. Workshop members then script their own scenes using material they have uncovered.

It was during one of these sessions that the idea for this book came up. Several members wished to take the experience further and write an account or short story based on their lives. We decided to put together this collection *CLEAN TIME*.

As a result of an advertisement in *Time Out* and *The Times Educational Supplement* as well as the attention of local London press, we received a surprising number of very good stories, half the senders preferring to remain anonymous. The selection panel found the overall quality of the work powerful and unique. The majority of the submissions came from addicts and very few from family members. Mothers of addicts we spoke to said that writing would be too painful. Addicts, on the other hand, found the process a 'release' and 'valuable', and many said they were glad of this opportunity to pass on their recovery message. The experience of writing gave a creative release similar to the workshop enactment. There were few stories about co-dependency (when a person's life becomes submerged in and totally dependent on another's life) and we were told that it is considered an unattractive addiction and no one wanted to write about it.

The accounts are presented first, the stories follow. 'Inner Void' describes the state of addiction, 'Tell Me' the actual territory of being high, 'Terry' the journey to being free. The writers, seventeen plus, some following successful professions now, mostly talk about the past. Two of the short story writers are not using personal experiences but their exploration and understanding of addiction.

In *CLEAN TIME* we want to share the sense of reality and discovery experienced by the writers of these stories.

Northern Bridge Productions

What is Co-dependency?

by

Patrice Chaplin

Co-dependency stems from the same place as other addictions and is more common than supposed. It is often mistaken for sado-masochism, but elements in the relationship are different. The victim is rarely masochistic but looks for fulfilment and warmth. This is not gratified through pain. The perpetrator, most usually male, cannot survive without controlling, so causes pain. He has often been abused as a child. The victim with too few boundaries and too much need for closeness is open to attracting a partner who needs to control and punish. He is often recognised as having a certain charm but low self-esteem.

The initial fix is his charm and the victim's submission. The bond is ecstatically complete. This too-good fit, the locked horns of symbiotic closeness lead to ever more dangerous roles. Trouble starts with an unexpected dart of criticism. The victim apologises, makes the necessary change and thinks no more of it. The criticism moves to something else and the victim changes accordingly – her hair, the tablecloth, friends, life. The criticism becomes abuse.

By acts of abuse and violation the perpetrator dominates his partner and so experiences a necessary sense of power. He can switch mood like spinning on a sixpence, all charm if an onlooker should appear. The abuse is private. The victim finds it unwise to go for outside help and tries to mend the situation herself. She keeps quiet.

After each crisis she clings to optimism. 'It won't happen again. I just have to get it right.' The perpetrator always blames the victim for his brutal behaviour. 'You asked for it! Look, what you made me do!'

The victim gives up friends, independence, choice. Stripped of every outlet, she becomes virtually kidnapped. This relationship for which there is no cure can lead to injury, breakdown, suicide, murder.

The perpetrator could have treatment including anger management, but he is usually in denial. The victim could escape to a safe place and start again, but often by this time there is no other place imaginable. The invisible prison bars, courtesy of the perpetrator, have done a good job.

The female perpetrator – on the increase both in heterosexual and gay relationships – is more elusive, as women are usually associated with nurture, care, mothering. The perpetrator, feasting off the substance of another, resembles a vampire. The victim, stretched to breaking point, becomes susceptible to archetypes from beyond the known and comfortable. Disintegrating finally, she would not be accompanied by a fully-fleshed partner but an essence existing in hints and shadows more lethal than a batterer's fists.

Each party is in search of wholeness. The tragedy is they both end in a state of destruction.

1. The Voices of the Battle

by

Michael S.

The promise

Anna gently pushed my ribs with the burning end of her first finger. One after another. Just to make sure that none was broken. 'You almost killed yourself, when you stumbled in the bathtub,' she said.

Something had happened last night: I had bruises all over my body but I must not recall anything. 'It was no water in the bathtub, that's for sure.' I tried a joke.

'Do you promise me that you will stop drinking?' she asked.

I looked at her for a while. I have never promised her anything I could not keep. From within myself I could hear the voice of my Mind: 'If you don't want to lose her, tell her now whatever she wants to hear!' I waited for my other voice, which I know would come. 'Steve, you are in no way prepared to keep this promise,' screamed back the voice of my Heart.

Too tired, I chose the easy way. 'I promise you,' I said.

'Call in sick today, stay home and look after yourself,' said Anna, and gave me a good-bye kiss. Before I possibly could change my mind she left for work.

The events of the evening started slowly to unwind. I did not trust my memory, so I started to follow their path. I must have been on the terrace, as always. Instinctively I touched my nose with my hand. It hurt. Had I forgotten again to open the large, heavy, glass sliding door? The glass was not broken. My nose neither. I was particularly happy to see that the pot with the red-violet petunias was still there. I've been struggling for weeks to capture their colours on canvas. Its twin pot did not make it through my last binge. I still could not remember anything from last night.

A lethal urge to face my colleagues and show them that I am all right and they are all wrong coincided with a wave of resentment against them.

'Today they will all see that you are committed and trustworthy. They will be sorry for the wrong they did to you.' My Mind was pushing the right button. Will they? I hated them all!

Suddenly my dizziness was back, so was my fear that I shall faint and die. What if my time is over? I started panicking. I did not want to die! My knees were shaking. I will not make it to the hospital, I thought.

'Take the medicine,' the Mind said.

'These feelings are not real. They are only in your mind. You promised her not to drink. I promise you, they will pass,' said the Heart. Yes, I promised, but if I die, it doesn't matter anyhow.

'You are only human,' encouraged the Mind. 'You need a jump-start.'

I went straight to my strategic drink reserves. They were depleted. Probably from the night before. Only one can of cider was left untouched. I opened it with care, but spilled half of the warm liquid on my shirt. The rest did the trick. The dizziness disappeared like the fog in summer mornings. A big relief flooded my body, followed by the joy of being alive.

I was ready to go to work.

Departing the trusted world

It was early in the morning and most of my colleagues were not in yet. I went through my mail as I did every morning. In my calendar I discovered a meeting I was not aware of. It was with my boss about personal issues. My heart started to beat quicker. I opened the letter attached to the invitation. It was the draft of a written warning for misconduct in the office under the influence of alcohol. Me – misconduct? It must be a bad joke from one of my pals. The worry about losing my job sneaked in and the resentments started to boil. It was not fair! I certainly was not drunk yesterday. In any case not more than in any other day.

'There is a conspiracy against you, Steve,' said my Mind.

What should I do now?

'Breathe,' said the Heart.

Breathe what? There was not enough air around!

'Go get it,' said the Mind.

This time I knew I was going to faint and die. I rushed out of the building.

'You never fainted in your life,' the Heart said, 'why now?'

'Because now you have a heart attack,' answered the Mind.

'Shall I show both of you how it is when I hurt?' asked the Heart.

Do it, I challenged her. Seconds later a knife straight into my chest taught me a different sort of pain which ignited a different sort of fear. I had to reach the emergency room of the nearby hospital before I lost consciousness.

At the traffic light in front of the hospital I had to wait. From all the shops around my eyes got fixed on the window of an off-licence. A small bottle of French white wine glanced back. I entered the shop. One of these bottles usually did the trick. Today I wanted to be on the safe side. I bought two. I opened the first one and looked at it. If it is really an attack it is not wise to drink, I thought.

'It is not wise to drink anyway,' said the Heart, while I was pouring the wine down. 'You are lost, my friend. And we are lost together with you!'

'What nonsense!' said the Mind.

At the reception desk of the emergency room at least twenty people waited to be taken care of. I smelled fear and sweat. I did not want to be one of them!

'Am I safe if I faint here?' I asked a nurse while completing the admission form. She didn't even look at me. I decided to wait outside. In the fresh air I felt better. 'We just overcame one of our major crises. Let's go back!' ordered my Mind.

In the office, my boss waited for me. 'It might have been only a perception yesterday,' he said, 'but if you convey this perception in the office one more time, we will be forced to take your trading licence back.'

I hated him. I hated him for all the good reasons of this world He was ugly, incompetent and perfidious. I could not possibly have been drunk from one glass of Chardonnay.

'You'll bounce back,' he said. 'I am sure.'

Bounce back from what? What was wrong with me?

'Everything,' assured my Heart.

'You are my hero, Steve, and you do not have to accept all the crap people throw at you,' said the Mind.

The last time

It was evening. Anna was not yet home. I felt the need to reward myself.

Will I have enough strength for a masterpiece? I grabbed my painting gear and started to play with the colours.

Becoming a painter was everything I ever wanted to do, till I discovered the money. And with the money came the obsession of having to make a career. I was not better nor worse than many others who succeeded. Then came the fears. They grew and became panic attacks. One day, I learned that alcohol could control them. But a drink alone was never enough.

On the terrace, as my thoughts were playing with the squirrels in the trembling poplar, my hand was spreading out colours on the canvas. But colours like thoughts, whenever I start mixing them absent-mindedly, come out a large brown spot. The canvas reflected the hurting reality again: I had no idea how to express myself in painting. Was it a mirror of my soul? I chased the thought away. I had to get a bottle of wine and try again. Deep in myself I had the strong belief that next time it would be miraculously better.

'Don't bother about not being perfect. You are not going to achieve either power or money with your painting, anyhow,' said the Mind and added after a while, 'If your will is strong enough there are no obstacles too big for you.'

Indeed, if I only could be more appreciated, if only people would stop hating me for doing the right things. I will become the old me again. This spiritual, sensible, gifted and modest person I used to be.

'Ha, ha, ha!' the Heart was laughing, 'the old you is gone forever, Steve, if he existed in the first place. You are as captive to the drink as I am captive to you. You are trapped within the bottle.'

I might be trapped in life, but not in a bottle.

By the time I finished the wine it was twilight inside and outside. I felt my Mind spinning slower and slower. He was tired as well. The chill of the night woke me up. I was still on the terrace. My painting gear was lying around. When I looked at the canvas I felt like I had bitten a lemon. The image of my artistic failure was more hurting than seeing Anna in the kitchen crying.

'Forget about the painting, you better apologise right away,' the Mind pushed.

'And offer her a way forward,' my Heart insisted.

'First she has to acknowledge your situation: unappreciated, misunderstood, pushed to the edge,' said the Mind.

'You are going to lose her,' added the Heart.

'We will find you another woman if she leaves you. There isn't anything that the two of us can't do, if we want it desperately enough,' said the Mind.

I believed it.

'You are both insane!' the Heart closed the dialogue.

I entered the flat. 'I am sorry,' I said.

'There was a time when you did amazing things only because you wanted them badly. Why can't you give up alcohol? What's the matter with you?'

I did not know the answer myself, so I walked away. She followed me into the bedroom. She was pale, tired and beautiful. 'I promise you to try,' I said, and was shocked how easy it was to lie this second time. I went straight to bed hoping that I would fall asleep at once. I did.

I woke up as usual in the last days, at half past one in the night. I was shaking too much to stay in bed. I went in the kitchen. Somewhere behind the marmalade jars should be a can of beer. I found it. The beer was sour but the effect was the trusted one. Anna appeared in the doorway and dragged me back to bed. This scene had repeated itself for months now. We were both tired of it.

I could not sleep. What if tomorrow I die? I was shaking. An urge to drink again became my master. My head was spinning. The only undiscovered bottle I could recall was concealed in the laundry basket. Anna's breath was quiet and slow. I closed the door of the bathroom with great care. The warm expensive French champagne was waiting for me.

When she came in, I was half drunk sitting on the lavatory seat. I expected a row, but somehow I did not care.

'You hate champagne,' she said.

'I still do.' My eyes were sparkling. She was so pretty. She was not prepared for a fight. I was relieved.

'We will talk tomorrow,' she said.

The first hours of the journey

It was one of these mornings when one knows something is going to be different today. She was watching me waking up. I smiled, but my smile passed through her eyes and didn't return.

'Are you mourning me?'

'It will be for you to decide,' she said. 'I just got an appointment for you to see a doctor. In an hour's time.'

'I don't need a doctor.' I need a cider, I thought. 'Today I feel fine, so far.'

She caressed my hair.

'I will give up drinking,' I said. 'I promise you. I love you.'

'I love you too, but I don't trust you any longer. I find it hard to believe that you can solve your drinking problem by yourself.'

'I hate my job, but we need the money. I only fight my panic attacks. I am totally unhappy with my life. I am a painter! The daily stress destroys the artist in me. The fear of dying is ever present. What do you want to know more?'

'You need help. After last night I know I can't help you.'

'What was so special about last night?'

'Everything.'

I tried to recall if anything else had happened which might have hurt her. 'Do you want to get rid of me?'

'If you don't get rid of yourself.'

Maybe she was not totally wrong, I thought.

After we left the main road we entered an illustration from the fairy tales of my childhood: a narrow uphill driveway with trees on both sides. A green tunnel. I never liked tunnels.

Fighting the denial

Where was I?

The answer came in the form of the nurse-on-duty, who took basically everything away from me except the books and my clothes: the putter, the shaving gear, every sharp object she could find in my bag, the aftershave, because it contained alcohol. The checks in the airports are a joke in comparison with this one, I thought. 'In the first week of the detox programme none of the above is permitted. Your partner is not allowed to visit you either. You will see her Thursday, at the Family Evening. If she attends.'

Detox? Me? What for? Was I intoxicated? It must be a mistake. I had better find out. I asked to speak to the doctor. It was too late. He was gone for the day. I returned to my room, shaking, dizzy and tired. I tried to read, but my head was all over the place. I was afraid to die in my sleep, so decided not to close my eyes.

'You are trapped! Run away! Save yourself.' My Mind was restless. 'Try to think logically. Try to think.' I could see where I was, but I could not think. The noise in my head was too loud. For the first time in ages I wondered what my Heart would say. She was silent. 'She let you down,' said the Mind.

Next day, the nurse introduced me to the group. My only desire was to get out of the room as quickly as possible. 'You certainly are not like them.' My Mind confirmed what I thought. 'Run away, Steve, run away!' Why do the others stay? I hoped my Heart would come with an answer. So many times before I tried to make my Heart shut up. And I could not. Now I cannot make her talk.

People in the room began to speak about themselves, one after another. Losers, I thought, who cares about losers? I solved all their problems in my head, but nobody asked me for advice. A middle-aged woman spoke about her anxieties and how she cured them with vodka. Was it possible that this woman experienced the same feelings as mine? Was I not the only one treating fears with drinks?

'Steve, do you want to share anything with the group?' somebody wanted to know.

'It's none of their business to know anything about you,' my Mind whispered.

I could have shared an experience I had in Regents Park some weeks ago, seeing a drunkard on a bench with a can of beer, spilling it all over. My can of cider was hidden in the pocket. When he asked me for a cigarette and I answered that I quit ten years ago, I saw a spark in his eyes.

His hands were shaking. So were mine. I was shaved and my clothes were clean, but the hell in our heads must have been the same.

I stood up and wanted to leave the group.

'Where are you going?'

'There's not enough air here.'

'Are we looking like suffocating?' asked a voice in the room.

'I feel like dying. It is the single biggest fear I have in my life.'

'We are all in here to save our lives, not to die, my friend.'

Time to change

It was Thursday evening. Family Meeting. The turmoil within me became almost unbearable. It will be the first time I meet Anna really sober. I was looking forward to seeing her. Is she still loving me? Will she leave me behind? Could she ever trust me again? How would my life be if she decides to go? Will I start to drink again?

The meeting started as usual: everyone introduced himself. Soon it would be my turn and I had to make a choice. My heartbeat was rising. 'Leave the room and never come back. She may not follow you, I will.' My Mind was as controlling as ever.

A strange voice banged in my head: 'Let's put it right, Steve. You are where you are meant to be. Everything you have done so far, good and bad, ended up here. If you want to change you must start by changing your Mind first.' Who are you? I have never heard you before.

The answer came in form of a light ache in the middle of my chest. I was relieved. My Heart changed her voice but was speaking to me again. Tell me, what shall I do now? 'Tell the truth,' said the voice of my Heart.

'Which truth? There are so many. You always had a choice of them,' said the Mind.

'At one single moment it is only one single truth. Voice it! Now!' said my Heart.

'My name is Steve and I am an alcoholic,' I heard myself saying out loud. A big laughter banged in my head. 'You are worse than clever!' yelled my Mind. 'You are going to spoil both your life and our party.'

Anna was staring at me. Her eyes were asking me whether it is true what I just said, or was it only to please the others.

'This is your last chance with her,' the voice of my new Heart was thundering.

'My Mind was not giving up. 'Steve, here is the deal: you walk out now and both of us start a new life. I will help you to change according to your will only.'

'He will drag you into hell,' said the Heart.

'What's hell exactly?' asked the Mind, sarcastically.

'Steve, hell is life within your private Bermuda triangle,' said my Heart.

'We have never been there,' my Mind pushed back.

'Oh yes!' replied the Heart. 'It is the space between the one you think you are, the one you want to be and the one other people see.'

'There are only gaps, Steve. And so far we certainly managed to close all of them,' interrupted the Mind.

'With alcohol!' replied my Heart.

I suddenly knew I wanted to change. I took Anna's hands and looked straight into her eyes: 'Yes, it's true. I am an alcoholic.'

'I am so proud of you,' she said.

'At least now, you know what you've got!'

2. Anti-Fear

by

Jeff Waters

The most intriguing bit of a fairytale for me is the last line. When I was a kid I wanted to know what happened the day after they lived happily ever after. I still do. The trouble with living in reality is that it goes on and on. No closing the book. A mentality that, courtesy of TV culture, is subdivided into movie-length periods of appropriate response doesn't fare too well with the unending. Enormous issues get tied up in half-hour slots don't they? If not, they certainly should. After a nearly two-decade-long saga of substance abuse followed by seven years of precarious and exhilarating sobriety, I felt I was owed a happy ever-after that meant something. In a super-real reality without bland respite, a break in the continuum can be something to yearn for. A long sleep. A happy ever-after? A full stop to the story of recovery.

What it was like, what we did and what we do today is a concept that suggests something is over and done with. A story with a beginning, a middle, and an end. 'My Sobriety – Done and Dusted' by Jeffrey James Waters. Yet there I am. Every morning my eyes open and I am back in the middle of an experience that doesn't have a conclusion other than the Big Check-Out. Today, for just this waking day I am sober, present in the moment (more or less) and prepared to take reality on the chin. The first few moments unfold and I force myself to exist. I bicker internally about rolling back into cosy oblivion or taking part in all that stuff out there again. Fortunately most mornings now a willingness kicks in and I participate. It wasn't always that way. How did I come by this strange set of affairs? What happened to turn this devout escapist 180 degrees into someone who doesn't mind getting up on a Monday, or a Tuesday, or a Wednesday? In fact, quite enjoys it. Each day is a life in itself, every night the bedroom waits like a crypt and in the morning we are reborn again.

Whether we like it or not. This penal arrangement has always inspired in me a sense of quite disproportionate dread. A claustrophobia with life you could say. I see myself moving through the boxes on a calendar as if they were a procession of locked rooms. The sum total of my coping skills when I first contemplated this monotony was to take stuff. Drink and drugs kicked the walls down and turned time on its head. Night became day and I slept whilst I was awake. The calendar got ripped up. So did everything else.

I cannot stress enough how much the addict is a victim of a condition. Sick, not bad. Afraid, not wicked. Whilst on the surface our behaviour does not seem to deserve compassion or forgiveness, we have to see that the street drunk is a damaged child twenty years later. A thieving junkie is a soul looking for love in a world that he cannot fully understand or feel part of. Addiction is a cry for help gone unresolved and no matter how paranoid and censorious the current regime, however hard an unenlightened judicial system tries to tell us differently via its tabloid mouthpieces, nobody is evil. The biggest crime any child can commit is naivety and the biggest sin society can commit is to condemn them. Addiction is a destination we all assist each other to reach. It's a place that we end up after everything else failed us. A place that we find ourselves, angry and perplexed, resentful, wounded and bitter. A place where other people and their customs no longer make sense. Head in hands we sit at the emotional baggage reclaim watching the same issues move slowly round and try to figure out when all the choices disappeared and when everyone else stopped caring. For some, other people never cared to start with. Surely, nothing we did could have prevented us from ending up in this place? How could it possibly be the fault of damaged children fleeing unlovable and unloved parents. What kind of Democracy order makes people stick needles in their arms? A domino effect of sickness, heirlooms of emotional damage passed down to the individual by an uncivil civilisation. Who is really to blame when the needs of the innocent are not met by the damaged? All of us.

Words and sentences appear in my head like branding-iron marks. You have to do it. You can't refuse. I MUST. I WANT. Seemingly, it had to end like this and the deeper our reluctance to end up here the quicker, for some reason, we arrive. Damaged people travel faster. We are escaping a pain and dread that can catch us up and my dread wears trainers. Eventually being on the run from yourself becomes exhausting so it becomes me and something wrapped in foil in a toilet cubicle in a city somewhere claiming my adult independence and 'power' back. Or a bottle made invisible by its carrier bag, rendered harmless by denial and a pretty label. Perhaps a social event that becomes an excuse for excess or any excuse for a social event. Leave me the vestiges of control while I lose it! Crowds are the only safe place to be alone. Bars and pubs have the kindest light through the typically unreal day, and are the only suitable venue to make my unfettered protest at the absurdity of life. Inside, nobody knows you like the fellow-wounded and nobody really cares about your unresolved pain. Thank God. Too serious! say the branding irons. Lighten up is the singsong between my ears as another drink goes down. All that pain is not really happening and I have as many choices today as ever I had. Damn it, I am here through choice, aren't I? On the other side of the room I am watching myself. I don't like what I see. He'll be right in my face about this tomorrow. But that's tomorrow and as we know, that is a lifetime away. Make mine a double remorse and soda.

Asking an alcoholic not to drink is like asking dust not to settle. We must be provided with an alternative at the very least as seductive as the habit we have to abandon. No self-respecting drunk would settle for less. We are in the business of highs and lows. The economy of satisfaction and misery is of great interest to us. Self-obsession is our devotion and a very strong argument against it is needed for permanent abstinence. (Psychic reprieves notwithstanding.) Thankfully, such a thing exists. An exquisite paradox which tells us by living in the moment we can experience deep, fulfilling liberty forever more. The sort of freedom that fills you with all the answers you're ever gonna need and tethers you lovingly to an instant universe that makes sense at last. Here, there is no beginning, middle or end. No regret or apprehension. No good boy, bad boy, just air moving in and out, eyes blinking, brain stopping for a lovely second or two. A state of Being so incomparable, so utterly powerful it's like stepping out of a film. A state I call Anti-fear.

There is no quick fix to fixing. The best I have been able to find is time. A few stolen seconds to begin with followed by an hour or two. Progress. An honest intention to grow and recover with a patient insistence that it will get better. Allowing the crawling clock to regulate your desires is a ritual that will grind you down. The twenty-four hour hamster wheel of obsession telling you it's too early for the next one, too soon after the last as you hurtle towards the inevitable self-hatred of going too far again. Again. Each day a new leaf that gets turned over, torn out and screwed up. Each day the heartbreaking resolve that tomorrow we will manage it differently only to ruin it again in a different way. It's no serious way to live, this hybridisation of desire and need. It grows like a new genus of emotion, it distracts us from our birthright and binds us with petty demands and whining concerns.

It's difficult to deplore oneself. A mental space like that has to be avoided at all costs as it cuts across the grain of what it means to be human and alive. However absolute substances may be in achieving a break in self-hatred it can only ever be a finger in the dyke. Truth is the long-term solution. Get honest about why you take the things you take. What do they do for you, truthfully? Addiction is thought. The idea that once this activity eased the pain of being an exile from Eden and if it worked once it will work again. Just for the record, 'working' is not trading penetrative sex in derelict houses for a share on a rusty hypodermic. Addiction is fond recollection replayed by the eternal optimists. A fancy definition of a lie. Those thoughts can be changed. They can be revisited at a later date, and even if it's only a second or two later I can guarantee it will have altered in shape slightly. It is the nature of thoughts to move like smoke and dissipate. That is fantastic news when those very thoughts can imprison us in behaviour and impulses so destructive as to kill us, rupture our families and denigrate our society. Nothing is static. Create time between the impulse and the act and you are actively winning. You will not have to sit on your hands for too long as the Universe supports positivism in all its forms.

Maintaining the all-precious buzz in its entirety is never going to happen. The froth goes off the top eventually. We all awake with disbelief that we grew up so ill-equipped and the world is such a complex place. On a real level life and death terrifies us all but we're here now and it's going to be okay. Self-destruction is no real solution and it's an awful waste of an experience that can be really interesting, beautiful and fun. We can all lay down our addictions and pain by telling each other what we feel. The moment those words leave your mouth and hang in the air in front of you they will have changed slightly and you will never have to feel exactly the same way about anything, ever again. At that point you are free and utterly in the moment. There is not a thought or impulse or addiction that can resist the force of the here and now and right now I am fine! How are you?

3. A Mother's Gift

by

Vi King

I was supposed to be called Samantha. I like Samantha but it wouldn't have suited me as a child for I had a lisp, which meant I couldn't pronounce my s's properly. It was no big deal except it could have been rectified with just a few sessions with the local speech therapist. I never went because my Mum had other things on her mind. Drink.

'It's the drink,' was the much-uttered phrase that passed from my angry mouth to the equally angry faces of my younger brothers and sisters.

'It's my only pleasure,' was the much-uttered phrase that passed from her resentful drunken mouth.

'I'm never gonna drink when I grow up,' we'd all say as we congregated in one of the bedrooms in what I now see was our version of group therapy; another reason we were upstairs was because the sofa downstairs had been wet by her as she had fallen into a deep sleep in front of the fire.

'Get down here and get to the shop for me ...,' she'd shout after waking up. The worst time was always after she'd woken up from a drunken sleep. Her once beautiful face looked haggard, dehydrated, spiteful – spiting herself. 'What do you want?' I'd ask, already knowing, as she fumbled around in her jeans pocket for a crumpled-up fiver, if she was lucky. 'Right, get me four cans of lager and twenty Berkeley,' she'd demand. I'd reluctantly take the money from her gnarled, nail-bitten hands, resentful inside at constantly having to run round after her.

Mr Patel always served me; the shops had been serving me with cigarettes and alcohol since I was eight years old. There were more off-licences on our estate than food shops. I hated it.

'When I grow up I'm leaving this dump,' we'd all say as we sometimes leant against an unbroken section of the garden fence, waiting for our Dad to get home so he could give us money to get our dinner from the shop.

'I'm never gonna drink,' we'd all say, as we kept our eyes peeled on the main road, waiting to catch a glimpse of our Dad's blue transit van.

'Your mum's an alky,' a few of the estate kids would shout.

'Like yours then,' we'd shout back.

'I can't wait to grow up ...' we'd murmur in unison.

'I wish I'd never had you kids, nothing but bloody trouble ...' she'd shout.

'You shouldn't have then, we didn't ask to be born.'

'Cheeky bleeders, you bring kids into the world and they don't thank you for it, if I had my time over again ...'

We'd run upstairs and laugh hysterically, it was like that, one extreme to another.

'I'm starving,' my younger brother would moan as he lay on the bed staring up at the ceiling, which displayed a large Guinness stain.

'Dad'll be home from work soon ...' I'd say, sitting on the carpetless floor, trying to will one of my almost daily headaches away.

'Do you think Mum'll ever stop drinking?' he'd ask, turning his five-year-old face towards me.

'God knows ...' I'd reply, wondering why God hadn't done anything yet, and then I'd reason that if God couldn't look after the starving Ethiopian kids why on earth would we be favoured?

And then the electricity would go out, which happened at least twice a week as a result of not buying enough tokens for the meter. We'd sit in the bedroom and wait, sometimes in silence, listening to her downstairs, usually talking to herself like she did in the early hours of the morning whilst everyone else was still in bed.

She was tortured. But we were too.

We'd look up at the sky through the dirty bedroom window, covered only by a once white net curtain and watch as the humid day came to a close, the light fading away as our stomachs rumbled.

'Wonder if Dad'll get us chippy,' my sister asked, looking up suddenly, her big eyes turning on each and every one of us, trying to infect us with her hope.

And then silence would descend again as we listened to *her* movements, an empty lager can being dropped on the kitchen floor, and then a few seconds later the familiar sound of another ring-pull ...

I wondered if it would be different if we'd had a mum like Gail's. She sometimes stood behind me in Mr Patel's shop, holding her mother's large shopping bag, waiting to ask for a bottle of Vodka. It looked so much better than lager, it was clear, like water, and I always thought the bottle looked so much more dignified and respectable than the horrible 45p cans of lager my mum drank.

'I'm never, ever gonna drink when I get older ...' I'd repeat to myself, as if trying to store up resolution for the future.

*

It was a bed-sit in Didsbury, the best part of Manchester, a million miles from the Moss Side council estate. It was a start. I felt such heart-wrenching guilt at leaving my brothers and sisters back there, with her, but they'd do the same one day, get up and walk out. I'd got a job at a five-star hotel in the city centre. I made friends. We'd go out at weekends. We'd have a few drinks. I preferred vodka. I wondered why some of my colleagues would drink lager, the very thought of it made me feel sick.

I always felt awkward trying to make small talk at the beginning of the evening, but I'd try and cover it up, appear confident, even though I felt like such an impostor. A few vodkas later and my spirit was free, *my inner spirit that is* – it never lasted though.

By the end of a Friday night, a whole group of us would stagger through the city centre, shivering as we made our way to yet another bar or nightclub. We'd always end up in the places that we said we'd never go to at the start of the night. A few of us would end up being sick, either in the back of a cab or on the street, we weren't fussy.

The next morning I'd wake up and for the first few seconds my heart would race as I asked myself what I'd 'done' the night before. I always remembered. As I lay in bed, my head spinning and my skin feeling like leather, I'd rewind the tape and carefully rake over each part of the night. Even if I'd not told someone what I really thought of them, or hadn't got into yet another argument, there was always that feeling in the pit of my stomach. I'd make my way into work. I could do that for the first few years, go into work despite feeling as though the world was wobbly. As soon as I arrived at work I'd try and ascertain what other people *really* thought of me by saying good morning and then trying to analyse their response, trying to determine whether or not they still liked me.

I remember asking one of my friends, 'Do you feel like, really horrible the morning after getting drunk?' She laughed and continued smoking her cigarette, 'God, yeah, it's called a hangover.'

But that's not what I meant. I knew what a hangover was. I just didn't know what *that feeling* was, it just sat at the bottom of my stomach, coupled with an overanxious mind. It's my Mum's fault, I'd tell myself. If she hadn't been the way she was I wouldn't have such an unhealthy attitude to alcohol.

I worked at the hotel for a couple of years, then one day I'd just had enough, not just of the hotel, which I felt was closing in on me, but Manchester too. I'd always dreamed of leaving but never thought I'd just get up and go. I was so scared, but I had such an overwhelming urge to leave. So I did.

I arrived in London with £40 in my pocket and a live-in job at another hotel. I stayed a week before leaving and begged to be allowed to sleep on the sofa of a man I'd met in a Manchester nightclub a few months before. He agreed. I stayed two weeks before moving into a room in South London. Then I started working in nightclubs in central London. Some of them were glamorous, or so I thought for the first few nights. We'd drink champagne and after work hit a few of the other West End clubs. 'If only they could all see me now,' I sometimes thought as a suited and moneyed middle-aged man bought me a glass of champagne. I never thought the same way the next morning though, as I usually woke up in a strange room. It always seemed like such a good idea the night before, liberating, *fun*.

And then I was at a 'glamorous' party where cocaine was being handed out. I'd been offered it before many times, but had always been too scared to try it, telling myself that at least I knew where I was with alcohol. The irony of it! But then I tried a line and that was even better. I felt so confident, not a care in the world. Now I could dream even bigger dreams. But after the first line had worn off I had to make sure I was standing next to someone who had some more. If only I could feel like this all the time, I told myself as the third line of coke went up my nose. I was OK, I told myself after the usual few depressing days following a regular binge, at least I wasn't addicted. I mean, addicts and alcoholics needed drugs and drink all day long. Didn't they? I never thought I'd end up with the same condition as *her*. My Mum was still drinking in the same old way. I'd been in London a couple of years and made a visit back to Manchester and naively wondered why she hadn't changed. My brothers and sisters were growing up quick and becoming more and more disillusioned and resentful towards life. I told them I was having a great time living in London and that as soon as they could leave home they'd be OK too. But I knew it wasn't true. The truth was I found life incredibly difficult. I was emotionally unbalanced, steeped in guilt and suffering from attacks of paranoia and panic. I had no idea how to 'do' relationships, but that's no surprise considering I only met men when I'd had a few drinks. They probably wondered who the real me was – actually they probably weren't too interested. If only I had known who the real me was. If only I could have removed the burden of my childhood off my shoulders, the shame. Did I mention the constant shadow of shame that hovered over me? It was more toxic than the drink and drugs put together.

I left Manchester feeling glad that at least I wasn't like *her*. Then I remembered the endless promises I had made to myself whilst I was a child, the dreams I'd had of leading a 'normal' life. Then I got to wondering how my Mum's alcoholism had progressed to where it was, because I had certainly seen how it had progressed within her over the years.

When I was a toddler she hardly drank. Then within a year or so, she'd have a 'quiet drink' in the evening after putting us to bed. By the time I was five it was every evening. At the age of eight she was drinking during the day and I was cooking and shopping. Then I was hit with the realisation that I *could* end up just like her. Despite doing things differently, drinking vodka and champagne to her lager, even smoking Marlboro light cigarettes, because she didn't. I even recoiled from some of her mannerisms with a vengeance, and yet I *was* the same. We shared the same condition. Alcoholism. That thing I'd always cursed and hated. The funny thing was I'd known since my first drink, known it wasn't normal to feel so different.

I called up a few friends and told them that I thought I had a drink problem. One of them said I was being stupid, I didn't drink all day or in the morning, so what was the problem, everyone had binges, everyone got drunk at the weekend and ended up puking all over their one-night stand and regretting it the next morning, said they'd never do it again and then repeat the same thing over and over again. *Everyone.* My problem, she said, was that I was hypersensitive, I should lighten up. I wondered if I should take the bit about being hypersensitive as a compliment. Then I started to rationalise: 'things will be different when I'm in a steady relationship, buy my first flat, learn to drive, buy a car, have enough money in the bank, start my own business, have children ...' And then another friend said that she noticed I never drank just a couple, and if I did manage to stick to a couple I'd get very irritable, and when I had more than a couple, which was most of the time, my character would totally change.

I was twenty-six when I sat in my first AA meeting. I still didn't really think I was a proper alcoholic, but I had been desperate to find some sort of a solution to my life. I sat in a crowded room full of people I didn't think could ever be alcoholics. I took an occasional glance up but mainly stuck to staring at my feet. I felt that everyone was looking at me, wondering who I was, why I was there. Then the meeting started, and a man, sitting at the head of a large table, started talking in a cut-glass accent about how he felt when he drank, *how he felt.* I felt stabs of identification like I'd never felt before, and then I realised this was me, he was me, everyone in that room, regardless of who they were outside the room, were all me, they all did the same things, they humiliated, degraded and tortured themselves whilst drinking. I felt a veil of isolation lift from my entire being that I hadn't known was there until it wasn't. This was the solution. It hit me between the eyes. There was no going back – I didn't want that back, no way.

Three years later I was sitting in one of my regular meetings, my younger sister sitting next to me; it was her first meeting. She stared out of the window. A year later we talked about our other brothers and sisters, it seemed obvious to us that some of them had this condition too. It's no wonder it's called a family illness. My Mum still drinks, it's a miracle she's still alive, considering the damage she's done to herself. My sister and I have both tried to get her to come along to a meeting with us, but her usual reply, even after all these years is: 'It's my only pleasure ...'

Some pleasure!

4. The Dark Side of the Moon

by

K.W.

I suffer from anorexia. I am now twenty-five years old and very simply, anorexia has robbed eleven years of my life. The diagnosis has now changed to atypical eating disorder due to the severity and duration of my illness, where I have developed and displayed almost every form of maladaptive eating disorder behaviours classified under anorexia and bulimia nervosa.

It is difficult to know where to start without putting in the punchline – twice my weight got so low, I nearly died, I had an out-of-body experience, vision impairment, incontinence. I was so weak that I could not stand or move a muscle and an alleged heart attack.

Writing this, it is obvious that I have recovered physically, but after the second out-of-body experience, was left scarred mentally. I had stopped sleeping for many months prior to this, not surprisingly, and as an out-patient, was water-loading excessively in a vain attempt to falsify my weight, by fooling the medical team and essentially trying to kill myself.

Well, I effectively did. I wrecked my chances of having a normal life again if my body were ever to be restored to full weight by getting so low, sleep-deprived and water-loaded so that the chemicals in my brain went haywire. It would have been simpler to have died than thinking about that terrible time, and the toll taken on my body resulted in a psychotic breakdown. The period of being on death's door from starvation compounded with a psychotic episode on an orthodox medical ward without any specialists, was frightening beyond belief to both those around me and, of course, to myself. Although remnants still linger six years on, nothing can compare to that crazed year. It was so awful that my family can't even bear to talk about it. A diagnosis and prognosis are difficult to make but I am still on anti-psychotic medication which, I have been told, I will have to continue taking every day of my life.

Psychosis has been a cruel side effect of my addiction. All I can say is that your body is not an invincible vessel. Severe eating disordered behaviours can result in extreme and dangerous consequences and you can consider yourself lucky if your recovery is only scarred with related psychological difficulties around food. It is rarely so clear-cut.

The worst thing now is that although I am successfully recovering from my eating disorder, being at the end of my longest hospital admission of two years and having been at target weight for one and a half years of those, the fear that I place in psychosis actually diminished my fear of my eating disorder. So, although I may seem recovered to people in that I eat three meals a day, I look and act healthily, there is still a dark side to my world. Stress, anxiety and tension are the three main beasts of my illness and are always prevalent as they are part of 'normal' living. The fear of not being able to cope is always there.

Let me explain properly. As a long-term insomniac, I have very hard nights. I find it difficult to get to sleep, to give myself permission to sleep, and when I eventually do, it is only for a few hours. I am scared of sleep and that is after a day's work of dealing with the recovery of my illness. Food and the thought of food is fought in the daily arena of life. I am a scared and nervous person, not just necessarily to do with food. I put this down to the horrendous experiences of my psychotic episode which may or may not have happened to me.

I chew gum constantly, from the minute I wake up. It keeps me feeling safe and protected and stops me from smoking excessively. Nowadays, I get through about ten packets a day but it has been a lot worse. Somehow, it stops me from thinking and worrying, so it calms me down and helps me to cope with my meals. This need for having something in my mouth goes back to the critical times in my life, where I was at my lowest weight and was not expected to live. To put it in its context, my life was at such threat that the highest amount of calories given via a naso-gastric tube were barely enough to sustain it. I was unable to chew because of the lack of muscles in my face and neck. My mother and father have both stood at my bedside supporting my head and neck while spoon-feeding me with soft food or 'Ensures' – high calorie drinks in order to save my life. I have been through a few periods when I have had to take in 15,000 calories a day with my weight just under 4 st. The normal amount for a woman is just 2,000 a day. My body was in such a process of deterioration that with even that amount of calories, I was unable for a while to gain weight.

I've just had my lunch and my head feels woolly. That for me means that my thinking is woolly. The whole process of experiencing the food in my mouth and stomach feels as if it is sitting on my brain. I am now chewing and feel angry. I need to feel clear. To me, you don't just feel hungry, eat and feel satisfied and are then able to 'move on'. You battle through the food and then afterwards feel uncomfortable and awful. It's relentless. Eventually the woolly, irritable feelings subside as I digest and then the process of building yourself up for the next meal begins.

I'm running on a treadmill, a 24-hour treadmill. When night comes, I don't breathe a sigh of relief and surrender into sleep. When I lie in bed, with the influences of people in my day receding, I lie in silence and the dark, a familiar place for me, and there is nothing to scare me or for me to do. I can then actually become me, distanced from my illness and it is then that thoughts hit me like a sledgehammer. What have I done with the day? What have I achieved? I have been hiding in my usual hell. Guilt floods through me but this time, not guilt about my eating disorder but guilt at my life. I would say that this is the only time that I am in touch with my true self. There are no distractions to keep me on the treadmill, on auto-pilot. But what can I do? Night stretches endlessly in front of me. I am caught between days. I think and reflect. I cannot sleep.

Another of my addictions is cigarettes. I smoke like a chimney and have a bad cough. I need my cigarettes in the night to dull the pain, dull the anxiety, dull my exhaustion. It lasts a couple of hours like this, anxiety rising in my chest quelled by a cigarette, reality stops. I start to panic about another day. How did I manage to maintain weight today, how will I manage to do it tomorrow? I have to look good for tomorrow, I have to appear perfect and coping so that I will be treated with respect and not with the prejudice that so often is meted out to the mentally ill. This, of course, is what in the end feeds the conditioned anorexic's obsession with their appearance and need for bodily perfection. The yearning to function normally and of course to attempt each day in order to achieve this, has to start with understanding of our illness and respect for us from others in society.

My days are literally 24/7 – they last 24 hours, from 6 to 6. Panic now really sets in, I feel as if my body stops, my eyes are crying at the knowledge of what I next have to do. I feel compelled to run down two flights of stairs to the kitchen, open the door to the fridge, take out the milk. I savagely rip open a cereal box, pour the cereal and milk into the bowl and sprinkle sweetener over it. If I'm resolute, I'll stow away with my bowl to my room, hoping the magic bowl will dissolve all my fears away by the time I have finished consuming it. Ah, the sweet milk, the munchy calming effect of the cornflakes! The magic has worked on a couple of occasions in the past so I feel I need to repeat this in the hope that it will erase and give balm to my pain. But hundreds of times it hasn't.

What actually happens is that I scavenge whatever I can find next and eat until I feel exhausted enough to purge and vomit. Only then does the sought-after sleep come to my ravaged body and mind. I reach then to what I come closest as my nirvana. Empty, violated by food, triumph and disgust cancelling each other out. I lie back, put some music on and with only a couple of hours to go before I have to get up, my mind feels pure and I drift off. This contradiction of my need for food and the connection to some kind of resolution and peace in order to be able to sleep is the main feature of my life at the moment. It feels normal to me, but yet I keep it a secret. I do not think of it as a serious problem. Anyway, who said that recovery would be a bowl of chocolates?

5. Diary

by

Kate S.

Bulimia thrives on your loneliness. The second feelings are felt, like molten lead bubbles rising up in your stomach, the impulse is to push them back down and deny them. Food is the perfect tool. Bingeing is a means to an end: the purge. In that moment you have expelled your fear; the fear of living for another minute, fighting through life. When your stomach has been emptied there's a sense of relief, because you have just seen your entire life flash before your eyes. It's as if you've nearly died, but you know you will always live. I believe that the addict is in a constant state of mourning for the death of the person they used to be, and/or the person they could be. Any potential whatsoever exists suspended in time.

When the hunger takes hold of a bulimic it's all-encompassing. Food becomes the focus for every drop of pain and fear in your life. When you're thinking about food you don't think about anything else. Nothing can touch you. No one can help. You feel like you're sitting in a goldfish bowl trapped, forever watching life happen to other people. Loving and live are things that other people do. The normal people. The land of the living is separate from the life of any addict. Because the feelings of worthlessness and self-loathing are so strong and real, it means that you can never feel loved. It's impossible to imagine that anyone could ever love this wretched, self-harming being. But of course, other people are always the last to know about it, to realise the true depths of your despair.

It took me years before even admitting to myself that I had a problem. Deceit becomes a huge part of everyday life. I longed to feel like a child again. Eating when I felt hungry, stopping when full, carefree, reacting naturally to sights, sounds and smells. Things change, events occur which force children to develop ways of coping with pain. They become adults, stifled by society's demands, concealing true feelings. Paradise is lost, and for some a nightmare begins. Somewhere along the line you stop living moment to moment and become detached from the pain of never being good enough, clever enough, pretty enough. ... For me, I always felt an overwhelming sense that no matter how much I learned about people, I could never really know anyone; never feel a true connection to life.

And that's the real problem. You're not really living at all when you've got bulimia digging its heels in 24/7. It's a disease, but like any substance abuse or addiction, it doesn't just affect your body, but it erodes your soul. It's a self-fulfilling prophesy, by which I mean you become all that you despise.

A friend of mine from a privileged background told me once how her brother stole silverware to fund his heroin addiction. Just the odd thing that they wouldn't notice for a while – silver cutlery, candlesticks and such like. For his family, of course, finding things were missing not only smacked of betrayal and cruelty, but just confirmed their worst fears – that he was jeopardising any chance of recovery to the advantage of his own demise. All he cared about in the world was heroin.

The sickness of addiction seeps into every part of your life. Hiding becomes a part of who you are. Trying to fund the addiction becomes increasingly difficult. Food would disappear from my parents' house at a rate of knots. My life became about eating secretly, and more importantly, bringing it up afterwards.

Relationships with people became impossible, out of reach until the day that you decide that you simply have to get better, or exist in a life in limbo, your body and soul rotting from the inside out. It becomes impossible to relate to the present when you are permanently tired and irritable. No one can touch you because you are a seething mass of self destruction. At its worst, I didn't leave the house for weeks on end, except to go and get food. Making yourself vomit up to ten times a day, sometimes more, turns you into a wreck. And maybe the worst part of it is that no one can help you. Because they don't know. And even if they did, the bulimic is a master of denial. Secrecy is paramount. This is one of the main problems with any addiction. It's one thing lying to other people, but it's the lies you tell yourself which put you in danger because you just can't stop. I was so angry with myself, everything and everyone. But it came over me in waves as if something inside me knew that if I let my real feelings manifest themselves,

I'd be overwhelmed. I'd been frozen for so long, I didn't know what might happen. That feeling was compounded by an overwhelming need to love and be loved. Whenever anyone had tried to get close to me, I was consumed with nausea. It seeped from my soul and infected my body. I hated myself so much because I thought – truly believed – that I could never really be happy because I was unlovable.

Having suffered from an eating disorder for so long, I am very aware that it can be hard for people to understand bulimia. They assume it's about losing weight. This is not necessarily an issue at all, which can be difficult for some people to fathom. In my case, I disliked being too thin for fear of drawing too much attention to myself. With bulimia, you are never not hungry. Even when you can feel the walls of your stomach screaming for you to stop, you continue to cram it fuller and fuller to breaking point, before the pay-off – the dizzying high. Like any addiction, your thirst is never quenched – the hunger never sated. The only comfort you have is the control over your own abuse.

You feel distanced from the rest of the world as if your life is going through a different filter to everyone else's. Addiction to food is a taboo subject in a society which fears and denies addiction. If someone is an alcoholic or a drug addict it's easy for other people to pigeon-hole them. But everyone needs to eat. It's so hard to define for the sufferer, even harder for someone who has never had an addiction. People with eating disorders are not some weird minority. I believe that society needs to change its perception of addicts before we can move on. Just because someone is addicted to food as opposed to chemicals doesn't mean it's less of a problem. Pain is relative and cannot be compared to anything. We only have one life and it's no good saying that heroin addiction is worse than food addiction. Despair, loneliness, hopelessness and misery are very real to whoever is feeling them.

At its worst my disorder made me feel like everything was happening in slow motion. Thoughts of suicide were regular, always just under the surface. The only thing that kept me going was the hope that tomorrow might be better, that I might have some control. Now of course, I realise that there is hope. That you can recover. Sadly, things often have to hit rock bottom before you pick up the phone and ask for help.

When I was asked to do this originally, I was going to read a series of diary extracts from when the bulimia was at its worst, but I found that too painful, and not very helpful. Instead I chose to write an overview of the way I felt. Sometimes my diary entries were nothing but angry tirades at myself, which I now recognise to be outlets of despair about not being able to control food.

It's important to think of bulimia not as part of the sufferer, but more as a parasite that uses you. The sufferer of any addiction feels disengaged from their life, therefore the ravages they inflict upon themselves spiral further and further out of their control. Addiction is a beast that lives inside you. This is not some lame excuse for overeating, this is a fact. After all, why do people self-destruct? The answer to this will continue to elude us until we change our perception of what addiction is.

6. Inner Void

by

Jeff Waters

I lived in a squat once and on one of the walls some bright spark had painted the slogan 'Drink and drugs are a crutch but life's a broken leg'. How heartily I agreed then.

Addiction is more than a compulsion. It's more than just repeatedly taking a substance to feel better. For some of us it's an instinct. As obvious as breathing. My own personal addictions were so profound that for the first half of my life I was not even aware that I was addicted. A nervous breakdown finally led me dazed and squinting from the coma of seventeen years of drink and drug abuse, to a place where I could meet myself at last.

I had never loved myself very much. I was born with an ability to be my own fiercest critic and, unsurprisingly, when I compared myself to the external world I always came up wanting. Addiction took up the slack. It was the entrance fee to some sort of peace of mind and I paid it readily. For years everything seemed to be going exactly to plan. I had stability, direction and time. I belonged to this floating rock, albeit uneasily. I was actually sanctioning my demise for the sake of pleasure, writing emotional cheques I couldn't cover.

Despair disfigures us internally. Each fresh torment (real or imagined) bonded me closer to the external helpers, the usual suspects such as drink, drugs, food, sex, money, power as well as a few novel ones like pain, egocentric lies, melodrama and fear. I would have addicted to tomato ketchup if I'd thought it would work. I became very good at reducing everything to an instant-hit powder upon which to inhale. Not to embrace addiction was like not embracing life and apparently (being too much of a coward to kill myself) I had no choice over that. To take nothing would mean living in the void again and the void sat outside with no sympathy for me at all. My biggest fear was not dying, but living.

Ultimately this fear proved to be my greatest ally. All of this behaviour resulted in taking me to a place where I was so frightened, so truly looking death in the eye that it called the bluff of my tragic and romantic fantasies. The road forked. One way said hope the other one said death. The instinct that brought me into the world made the decision for me and I entered recovery. I had been given the gift of desperation.

7. Fantasies

by

Peter James Spite

'Hey!'

I heard this voice come from out of nowhere and it penetrated ... right inside ... right deep inside me ... A voice in the emptiness ... almost like she was speaking to me ... soft ... warm ... caring ... and I was so cut off from the people around me right then, as we sat there avoiding each others attention in our own little worlds.

I just heard it come from out of nowhere ... when I was sitting there in ... so much ... emptiness.

I looked up to see where her voice was coming from.

It was Mel coming through the speaker system in the bar, and it reached through inside me.

'Hey! ... don't you worry ...'

I didn't think anything could still reach inside there ... into that emptiness, that emptiness left now she had gone. Surrounded by these invisible walls of ice and inhumanity ... It was the first time a woman had touched me in so ... long.

It seemed like I heard her everywhere I went ... Everywhere I went someone seemed to put her on the jukebox.

I started to live ... just to get up in the morning to go to a bar and hear her voice again and ... It ... it became everything ... almost ... like the air I was breathing.

That voice ... it became more real to me than anyone else right then ... touched me inside.

'Don't you worry … Everything's all right you know …'

It just filled me inside with beautiful warmth.

It filled me inside … the warmth of the beer in my stomach and that beautiful voice … made me feel like … somebody was touching me again. I never wanted it to end. I just kept putting money in the jukebox and she was there again … Those first few notes soothing out through the air and around my body … and every time I heard them I knew Melanie's voice was about to come.

She became everything that I was … only it wasn't real … and in the gap between here and reality I started to destroy myself so that it could feel like real love.

… and I had to drink to make everyone … everything else fade away, so it was just 'me and her' … nobody else intruding.

To dissolve the contents of reality in the contents of that glass at the bar …

'Just one more … '

'Just one …'

But that one more is never enough … because it's not the alcohol that you want. It's the coldness of the reality around you that you don't want, and the alcohol is a way to walk away from it.

But that reality doesn't go away. It's still there when you've drunk that 'one more' glass. It's still there. Nothing's changed … nothing's fixed … nothing's solved … nothing's improved at all. And if it has changed then it's changed for the worse. Things don't often get better if you leave them.

It's still the same as before. Still the same as you left it. So you need another … and another … and …

It's never just 'one more'.

One more is never enough.

That reality is still there! It's still always there and that reality is Cold! Icy … freezing … Cold!!

The alcohol is a way to walk away, but only for a while. You always have to come back.

It's not the answer!

It's never the answer.

The answer is to fix what's wrong with reality! Only ... it's not always possible to do that.

Like when you lose somebody you love.

But you can't stop loving them just like that. It doesn't work that way and ... sadly ... that pain is the price you pay for being able to love.

It's the price you pay for being able to love somebody ... for being able to feel those feelings ... for having that capacity inside you. This is the inescapable flip-side of the coin ... and you just have to go through it until it's over. There's no avoiding it. Not if you really loved the person.

And it's the worst hell that was ever invented. You just have to accept it for as long as it lasts ... and hope that it doesn't last too long. I've seen people crushed by it ... and it's not pretty or romantic. You can see it in their eyes ... like a tortured soul crying out in pain.

And right then you stop caring about consequences, because when pain gets that bad ... you just reach out for any way to kill that pain ... any way! Any way at all.

You know ... Depression is like stumbling blind through a tunnel without end ... without light ... without hope. You can't see a way out. You can't see a future. All you see is darkness without end ... and you keep stumbling forward in the dark like a blind man ... just living in hope for a light shining in the dark. Sometimes if you can hang on then you can suddenly turn a corner and there it is! A way out with daylight streaming through.

But not always.

Not sometimes.

Sometimes that doesn't happen and as the darkness through which you walk continues then your mind starts to project images in the darkness ... on the walls around you. A desperate need to create some sort of reality.

Except those images aren't real.

The mind can't stand darkness and emptiness ... so it fills the darkness with dreams ... memories ... fantasies.

Except after a while those images of dream and fantasy assume a reality in your mind that they shouldn't, and your reality becomes formed out of delusion and hallucination. The unreal becomes real ... the unnatural natural. You become like a lost spirit wandering through dark, deserted corridors and where life has become no more than pictures projected onto the walls around you ... flickering patterns of light and life ... but if you try to touch them then your hand just passes through onto the cold stone they're projected on.

And there is always a price to pay ... a real price to pay for ignoring reality, because ...

Reality doesn't like to be ignored.

'Here it comes again ... Filling my soul, never want to let go'

'Hello?'

'I needed to talk to you ... I think I've done something bad to myself. I've just been through a relationship break-up and I've been drinking for days.

'I just start the minute I get up in the morning, and I think there's something wrong ... inside. I think there's something wrong inside my body ... I think it's alcohol poisoning.'

'What's your name? Give me your phone number and I'll get a nurse to call you back.'

'No, please don't! I did this to myself. It's alcohol related. It's my own fault ... I did this to myself!

'I shouldn't be ringing you.'

'Don't hang up! We can get a nurse to call you back in fifteen minutes. You're next in the queue.'

'No ... it's OK. I'll be OK.'

8. My Drink and Drugs History

by

Duke Roberts

My drinking propelled into orbit when I bought a crate of Teachers whisky at the tender age of fifteen. I was already consuming a bottle between two to four hours in conjunction with as many joints of marijuana I could afford. That crate of whisky lasted less than a fortnight. My drinking was mainly restricted to night-time activity to begin with, at various nightclubs and parties which I attended on a 24/7 basis. However, I smoked marijuana constantly throughout the day and night. I believed that the more I drank and smoked the more I commanded the respect of my friends and acquaintances. Consequently my urge to drink and smoke marijuana became relentless.

This pattern of heavy drinking and drug smoking was constant throughout my teenage years and my only moments of abstinence occurred when I was imprisoned for robbery, which in retrospect was drink and drug related.

I experienced my first blackout at twenty-one years of age when I almost killed someone. That event appalled and horrified me and evoked an unforgettable and irrepressible feeling of guilt, shame and remorse, which prompted me to cease drinking alcohol immediately. I was perplexed by the fact that I had no conscious recollection of the incident and was grateful that I escaped criminal charges. The cacophony of emotions that erupted inside me filled me with so much fear of losing control that as a result I abstained from alcohol for about ten years. However, I continued to smoke marijuana through the rehab process. I became aware of the fact that switching from one drug to another is called cross-addiction. Such an unfortunate predicament meant that any attempts by me to abstain from all drugs seemed almost insurmountable. My awareness of cross-addiction came much later on in my life, so at the time I was switching from one drug to another I thought I was being smart. This apparently led to my development of a cocaine habit later on.

By that time, I was involved in drug dealing and served various sentences for it. I was proud of that profession since I came to believe that I was no longer being dishonest. I thought I was doing a great public service and with all the abundance of money that flowed into my life, I glamorised drink and drug use with prestigious cars, expensive clothes, first-class travel and accommodation, expensive restaurants and womanising. I was also generous to others in the financial sense.

I came from a spiritual upbringing seeded and nurtured by my Mamie (my grandmother), and was acclaimed as academically bright from the age of three. My grandmother introduced me to God and prayer and taught me to fear no one. She caused me to have my one and only experience of unconditional love and cultivated me to respect everyone regardless of race, colour, creed or disability. My life was now contrary to all that. I blamed my mother for treating me as a domestic slave and my father for violently beating me on an almost daily basis and, furthermore, for denying me a university place when he compelled me to abandon my O- and A-level exams for low-paid jobs I resented. Further rejection resulted in my leaving my parental home at fifteen and consequently I became defiant and rebellious in society but thought my transformation was justified.

A marriage made in hell fuelled my alcoholism and drug addiction to greater depths of depression and despair. But at the time I thought it helped to relieve the pain, frustration and anger I felt about being trapped in a relationship with a cold, loveless and constantly callous, critical and nagging wife, who conceived twins within a few months of our marriage. Leaving would have been easy had it not been for the twins, hence I sought constant refuge in drugs and alcohol.

I had two failed relationships behind me which produced five children between them, but somehow I managed to give all my seven children emotional and financial support. My conscience, common-sense and a sense of responsibility caused me to go to great lengths to disguise my heavy drinking and cocaine habit (including crack smoking) from all my children. But I smoked marijuana in their presence since I thought it was harmless. However, later on, life taught me that I was wrong to uphold such an attitude towards cannabis, whether it was herbal or cannabis resin.

My reasons (excuses) for alcoholism and drug addiction kept multiplying. Alcohol was socially acceptable. Alcohol relieved me from insomnia, brought me down from crack and cocaine highs, enhanced my sex life, boosted my confidence, curbed my depression, assisted my social intercourse and generally relieved me from the pressures of life, emotional pain, guilt and shame, regret, anger and many more negative thoughts and feelings that also included paranoia. It was me against the world and the world against me. Often the majority of people I gravitated towards were drug addicts and alcoholics.

Drink and drugs became an obsession and I became their slave. In fact, I abandoned my businesses as restaurateur, club owner, music producer, songwriter, singer, poet, author and distributor of electronic games and pool tables as well as drug dealing, to concentrate solely on drinking and drugging. By the time I left my wife and twins, with a large luxurious house and all its contents paid for, I was a very tormented soul, and totally blind and insensitive to the fact that my life was on a downward spiral, spiritually, mentally, emotionally, physically and financially. However, drugs and alcohol were fooling me into a false sense of security, saying that everything would be all right. I'd wake up and things would be worse than the day before, but that deadly concoction of alcohol, marijuana, crack and cocaine imprisoned me in a world of delusions of grandeur, dishonesty to myself and to others, violence and disregard to all my responsibilities.

I lied and stole from my mother, stepfather, Mamie, my friends, and I lost my principles, moral value and integrity. I regularly denied myself food for the mind and body and spiritual food for my soul, through prayer and meditation with God and the great wonders of Creation. I fled from sleep for up to five days and nights at a time via crack and cocaine. At other times sleep became a wonderful and great escape from reality. I wished I could sleep forever and live in my dreams, hence every time I awoke I ran to King alcohol and cocaine (crack) whilst marijuana, which I thought would have always been my first drug of choice, remained on the back burner as a reserve when cocaine and alcohol were absent.

My life was agony, filled with suicidal thoughts like jumping in front of a moving train or into the river Thames from a choice of bridges.

I ended up in hospital twice for overdosing on one occasion from thirty temazepam capsules washed down with a bottle of vodka and twelve pints of Guinness after a heavy crack-smoking and cocaine-snorting session. The other occasion involved a bottle of amphetamines and several bottles of wine.

I kept denying I had a problem even after I wasted a vast fortune on drink and drugs, hotel bills, nightclubs, fancy restaurants, expensive clothes and hangers-on, otherwise known as fair-weather friends, as well as many women.

Financial poverty didn't deter me and I maintained my expensive habit of champagne and cognac by shoplifting them for my personal consumption as well as my crack habit. I still bathed and dressed in expensive clothes and splashed on expensive eau de toilette, but I was trying to fool the public into thinking my life was manageable. In fact, it was totally unmanageable and I was an empty shell.

Consecutive jail sentences for shoplifting didn't deter my habit, which resumed the moment I was released. I constantly denied I was an alcoholic and a drug addict to the probation service, the police, my lawyer and to myself. I was riddled with guilt and shame and feared what the world would think of me being an alcoholic/drug addict.

I refused to submit to the fact that I was beaten and as a result I declined the help offered to me by the probation service regarding rehabilitation. Consequently, I repeatedly went to jail for drug and alcohol related offences.

Eventually, I was evicted from my home for rent arrears and my first reaction was to leave all my possessions in the flat and seek refuge, comfort, false hope and broken promises from a bad spirit in a beautiful bottle and a false spirit in powder and crack cocaine. I was advised to attend the homeless persons unit in order to get assisted into a B&B, but I chose to go to a crack house instead. I hid the fact that I was homeless by simply saying to the legal tenant and crack dealers that I was head of security and would remove anyone who misbehaved from the premises.

The flat was infested with cockroaches in every room, and the bathroom/toilet was so filthy that I preferred to use the pub toilet across the road. However, this wasn't always practical and I was compelled to use it on occasions. I lost weight dramatically, and for the first time in my life I failed to have a bath for nearly a fortnight. In desperation for personal hygiene I scrubbed the bath and toilet bowl with huge amounts of bleach, soap and disinfectant. The fact remained that my life was a filthy mess, which no amount of bleach and detergent could efface.

All the things that I said would never happen came to haunt me. I was financially broke, homeless, estranged from my family and friends, living in a crack house and very distant from my God. I found myself begging and conning money from the general public and often reduced to secretly picking up dog-ends from the streets, which I made up into roll-ups.

From the depths of hell, agony and pain of my existence I cried to my God for help only to find his response came in another prison sentence.

In fact, in retrospect, that prison sentence on New Year's Day saved me from living on a park bench. Whilst in prison I attended my first AA meeting and was horrified and filled with disbelief when I realised I'd have to attend AA meetings for the rest of my life, since there is no cure for drug and alcohol addiction. I knelt down and prayed in my cell and admitted to God and man (including myself) that I am an addict.

Originally, I was a confident person and drugs and alcohol had eroded all my confidence and, as a result, I found myself drinking and drugging to regain the confidence I had lost. That confidence was false and expensive to maintain in the mental, physical, spiritual, emotional and financial aspect. Now my newly found confidence in God was and still remains the real and true confidence which lit my life with the fire of truth, honesty to myself and to other people.

From that reality, I grew strong and became willing and ready to face life on life's terms, and that meant that I was ready to do all that was necessary for me to live a clean and sober life. I found myself admitting defeat, something that I was adamantly reluctant to do in the past.

I tried to control my drinking and drug use over three decades via many methods such as restricting drink and drugs to weekends only, or only at night, switching my brands and types of alcohol and abstaining from one whilst using the other. I failed dismally on all counts and many more.

My resolve to stop drinking and drugging was just as abysmal. For example, I thought I would go out with women who didn't drink or take drugs, only to find myself doing so in isolation. The same thing happened when I thought I could stop by avoiding my friends with drug and alcohol misuse, but it was all to no avail. I was baffled and bewildered by my constant lack of willpower to cease and was relieved to find my God performing miracles in my life.

The first miracle was when I actually felt a sincere desire to abstain from drink and drugs. God answered my prayers by actually eliminating my negative pride and as a result I asked people for help and found that there was no shame in asking for assistance and that my fear in acting in that way was completely unfounded. Furthermore, my prayers were answered when I was admitted into a rehab centre the very day I was released from prison. A prison drug worker actually accompanied me to the rehab centre since I was honest enough to admit that I didn't trust myself to travel to the centre alone, since there was no guarantee that I would resist the call from King alcohol from the many off-licences along the way.

Once I had that first drink, stopping would be impossible, since I had to have more and no amount was ever enough, and my drinking always inevitably led to crack smoking which eventually led to more dishonest and criminal acts which always ended in a prison sentence. That dead-end road was no longer an option.

Now all the energy I used in my efforts to feed my habit are channelled into my recovery via the rehab process and the twelve-step programme which I ardently and instantly embraced. I find regular attendance at AA and NA meetings gives me strength and hope and a new circle of friends. Personally, I submitted to the fact that my old friends and behaviours were not compatible with my recovery and I thank God I had the courage to let them go. Being in touch with my feelings as well as facing life on life's terms is an exhilarating experience for me in recovery. There are trying moments, but I am aware that I have a choice not to use, and the consequences of my addiction as well as my desire for a clean and sober life easily prompts me to say No on a daily basis. Consequently, as long as I maintain a sincere clean and honest effort in my recovery, my God does for me what no one else can. Psychology failed, psychiatry failed, hypnosis failed, the medical doctors failed, acupuncture failed, imprisonment failed, my ex-girlfriends failed, and even I failed to remove my desire for drink and drugs.

The power that removed my desire came from God, and that is a miracle.

9. It Started with a Spliff …

by

Odunlamy Seté Olu

I was so clever back then. My ego knew no bounds, nor my rebellious nature. It was only the pain, you see, in the twelve short years I'd been alive. I'd been abused mentally, physically, sexually, emotionally and spiritually. There was no peace in my life and no love in my home. But I knew best!

With my mates, I walked the streets; hung out on the estates, showing off to the girls. Life was fine and all that had happened to me in that short life really didn't matter. It's just the way it was! The buzz of the first spliff took me away. The pain was gone! The excitement of the illegality and the heightened sense of awareness – I knew best! I was violent, like my Dad, and as skinheads, we'd have rows with rivals. Thieving was great, when you got away with it! By the time I was fifteen, I'd done two years inside and on my release, was respected even more as I'd go further than my mates, who always egged me on. But I knew best!

The pain was still there, and I was creating more and more. But I lived up to my reputation, and on my eighteenth birthday, I tried smack. Heaven! I'd found heaven! I felt like I knew I should. Just a little pin-prick from a 1ml worked and I didn't care. Wrapped up in my bubble, I'd do anything. As the years rolled by, I went into crime, mainly to supply my drug habit. I didn't care, and neither did anyone else! A few people tried to talk to me, warning me of the dangers of where I was headed. But 'what the fuck did they know?' They'd never touched a bit of gear in their lives, and they certainly didn't have the shit life I'd had. And anyway, I knew best!

In and out of prison; crime and habit getting worse; so fucking hard, I felt I would burst. But the respect it produced – 'He's a fucking nutcase! Don't fuck with him, he did this! He'd have the bottle to do it!' And I would, 'cos it made me feel good, and, of course, I knew best. Friends started dying, but there was hardly any crying. We'd grieve by getting smashed. 'This one's for him!' we'd say as we put our own lives on the line

My eighteenth birthday present was a screw opening the cell door in Ashford, when it was a remand centre, and saying: 'Happy birthday, son. You're off to the big house (Wandsworth). Now you're a man!' I tried not to give a fuck, but on arrival, seeing the grimness of the place, I must admit, there was no smile on my face. Walking through the wings, screws doing their best to humiliate and intimidate, while you carry your bed-pack and piss-pot. Seeing the older cons, some real tough. 'He's doin' 15rec!; he's doin' 10!; he capped some guy in the nut!' Such good role models! But you're a live wire – you quickly wise up. The first person to fuck with you, you take out 'the game' – PPQ battery in a sock! See some mates in the yard, they hook you up with some puff – 'shit, this ain't so bad!' Waiting on visits: your girl comes up. You're dying for sex and she's looking so fit. The only release for that is some degrading porno magazine that's been round the wing a dozen times. But I still know best!

On your release, wrecked in an hour. Back to the lads – it's party time! The cycle continues: drugs, crime, prison, and the years roll by. Then one day, the novelty wears off. Most of my friends dead, including my elder brother and my mother, both while I was inside. Funerals in cuffs hardens you up! But you begin to feel isolated, desperate, alone. The word 'alien' comes to mind. And suddenly, you find, even with people who still want to know, it's hard to relate or communicate. And resentment sets in; you become bitter. You resent the normal, good people, the ones who paid attention in school, who have good jobs, who are married with kids, cars and holidays. Okay, their lives aren't perfect. But from where you're standing – on a filthy stairwell, waitin' for 'the man', sweating 'cause you're sick and wearing the same clothes you've had on for a week – tell the truth … who would you rather be? But still, I knew best.

Hardly any friends now. They're all dead. But still I walk the earth, like some spectre. Now carrying guns; a time-bomb ready to blow! No fun anymore. I find it hard to smile. All the 'juice' I've had, I'm scared to look inside, so I continue. But now I seek oblivion. Living on the edge, rock getting to your head; finding it hard to look people in the eyes; emitting dark vibes to disguise all the pain you're in. But still, I thought, or I tried to, that I knew best.

I'd made my bed and laid on it – sick as a dog, dodgy and 'wired to fuck'. With psychosis setting in, you shun daylight, unless it's to 'score' or 'make a raise'. I do remember some of the days, but large chunks of my life are blank. But I only have myself to thank. For I knew best!

By now, I'd done twelve or more years inside. Nowhere to hide. Even after an acquittal on a robbery charge, I still went back to it all. Smack, rock, methadone, valium and temazepan. An excellent combination to dull the pain. But somehow, it didn't do the job anymore.

The few good people who had stuck by me throughout were getting tired of the same story. The 'borrowing' money, the lies, the 'I'm going to give it up this time!' When you're in the nick and they've taken time off work, out of their own stressful lives to visit you. Five 'O' kickin' in your door. I didn't feel up to it anymore. But I tried, even though I now doubted, I knew best!

Upon waking one morning, I'd run out of money – not sick, but opening my eyes to two mates 'fixing'. Claret everywhere, I had a moment of clarity! 'I'm in hell!' It was as simple as that. I got up, said, 'I'm off! I've had enough of this shit!' They laughed and said, 'OK! See you later, Rich!' But they didn't. I walked away, went to an ex-girlfriend's sister, who had helped me through all my using, and asked if I could stay. She agreed, even with a young baby. I handed her the 9-inch knife I was carrying, and went through a month of agonising. Checking with nothing but my willpower. But I did it! I was clean. It was like being reborn. Suddenly, lust for life! And lust for women, wanting to shag every girl in sight!

Nine years clean, and after a traumatic break-up of another 'relation-ship' I went into therapy after an emotional breakdown. I was told I was a 'love addict', using women like drugs; diagnosed 'borderline personality disorder' and 'traumatic stress disorder'. I thought only war veterans suffer that. But as I cycled away from my therapist's, I realised, I'd been through the war! I'd fought longer and harder than any war has ever lasted: 38 years. All the abuse I'd suffered had taken its toll. I felt like that little child – vulnerable to the extreme. People trying to manipulate you because you've fallen from 'grace'.

I relapsed. Eight months of hell and thousands of pounds later, I am again coming off. This time through detox. I am too old for this shit! Trying to find myself. Feeling like that little abused child, so fragile and vulnerable, in this big world that is going to the dogs. However did I think I knew best? My life in pieces – trying to climb back in, live peacefully, take responsibility. Not hurting anyone; not hurting myself. My beautiful fourteen-year-old daughter, whom I lost to adoption – what the fuck do I tell her? How can I make up for all I've done? Learn to love myself. I am on a mission to purify my soul, redress my karmic balance. The only goal; being humble, gentle, good and kind. Trying to love all and trying to find all I have lost.

In humility you find an acceptance of a kind and take things day by day. You, the main casualty of your karma, all the people you have hurt along the way. Because you were not given love, you fought so hard. Because you were hurt, you hurt others and yourself. Because you had a fucked-up childhood, you fucked up your life. It's the same for everyone! We are all just souls who want peace and love, and the world we live in is a reflection of the internal individual turmoil and destruction.

Neil Young sang, 'every junky's like the rising sun'. I hope my sun will rise, because when all's said and done, it hasn't been much fun. We all need to wake up – addiction is endemic in the world today! God bless our souls!

10. Living with Addiction

by

Elizabeth Hamilton

There is so much written about the various forms of addiction – addicts: their problems, their trauma and their demons. For their families, their loved ones, the ones they turn to, there are groups, self-help books and the medical profession – to get you through; to help you deal with the problems and issues; the way to deal with the illness that is addiction.

The reality can be very different. Living and dealing with addiction – having it part of your life. Nothing can prepare you for that. I am a relatively ordinary person. I have a home, a relationship, a young child and a career. Just a general, run-of-the-mill average person. But my life in the last four months has been far from normal. My husband suffers a form of paranoid psychosis. A marijuana-fuelled fantasy life, imbued with all kinds of bizarre beliefs. And he can also be partial to a drink, even though he readily admits to being an alcoholic.

He suffered such incidents in the past, something I'd always been aware of. But I thought that part of his life was over. He's better. Things are different now. His priorities have changed and he has responsibility in his life. Why is this happening again, turning our whole family life upside down? A one-word answer: addiction.

I'm the first to admit that I am often angry about the situation. Why? Why? Why? He should know better, I sometimes think. After all, he's been there before. Then comes apportioning blame. Is this all my fault? Was I too caught up with my job? Too busy trying to balance my life to notice what was slowly coming out of place? Or did I drive him to this state? I can be a bit of a cleanliness freak and my working hours are often unsocial. And I know I can be a right moody cow sometimes. Is this all my fault?

Of course, there is the worry. Will he ever be okay? Will we get through this? How is all this going to affect our child? Will I be okay? So many questions, I could go on forever. But there is always the answer: it is the addiction. Yes, we're back to that! No getting away from that one. It has affected all our lives, every day, 24/7.

Our frequent visits to the psychiatrist are meant to help. And they do, I think. But sometimes, the things that come out in those hour-long sessions, the 'mad talk' and his constant exasperating denial, leave me wondering if anything will ever be okay again. I've often found myself, sitting on that rocking chair, crying with hysterical laughter – not because the situation is funny (far from that), but because it really gets to the stage where I am feeling a little bit 'mad' myself. I suppose it's better than actually crying, but then I've done plenty of that too.

Medication can work, apparently. But then, it's only good if the person is willing to take it and carries on taking it until told otherwise. My husband likes to self-medicate himself. He seems to think he knows better than any doctor what toxins he should put in his body and for how long. It took us a while to realise this. Initially, he was quite open to their benefit and took them for several weeks. Then after 'a dream' one night, he stopped them. Of course, we didn't know this initially. As far as we were concerned, he was doing his best to get well. It soon became apparent what was going on, and before we knew it, he was drinking every day and sneaking out for the odd spliff. It was at this point where I really had had enough. Could he not see what this was doing to himself and his family? Apparently not. He literally had to be dragged back to the psychiatrist. He said he would not take any more tablets as the 'dream' had told him they would turn him into a vegetable. Suggestions that dope and booze would do this for him instead did not wash. We encouraged him to go to AA, but he was having none of that either. At this point I really was prepared to leave him. I could not see a future for myself or my daughter with this person I could barely recognise. His deception and his denial had pushed me to the edge. This fear of separation made him accept the medication; most begrudgingly. He said I was blackmailing him. I told him I was making him face facts. I would have left. It would have been the most horrendous thing to do, but I was quite prepared to do it. I know it is the addiction that has brought us here, and he is ill because of it. But there has to come a point when every addict must accept help, or face the abyss.

It has been so hard. Much harder than I often allow myself to believe.

I am a strong person, I know that, but it doesn't make it any easier. When you see your world crumbling around you, how would you feel? You deal with things day to day, the best you can, but when you sit and think about everything, even for five minutes, you get jittery. And when you see the effect it has on those closest to you, you accept the real consequences of it all.

Four weeks later and he has not indulged himself in any substance. But I am always on the alert – checking for glazed eyes, smelling for alcohol, monitoring his movements discreetly. He continues to take the tablets, albeit in a smaller dose than has been recommended. This he resents more than anything – he hates having the medication because he thinks he doesn't 'need' it. We are at the psychiatrist twice a week. This infuriates him as well. He sees it as a waste of time and money because everything is 'fine'. Basically, my husband has a problem with accepting the whole thing. He refuses to give himself over completely to this recovery process. He refuses to see the problem. I worry about this constantly. If he will not, or cannot, deal with the reality of the situation, is there any hope? I know he is still paranoid, maybe not to such an extent as before, but it is still very much there. And I know he struggles with his abstinence, but refuses to admit it. I try to be positive – he is, after all, taking the pills, and he does go to the doctor, despite his protestations. Things will be okay? I hope. All I know is that I can do no more than what I am already doing. At the end of the day, he knows what is at stake in his life. I just hope he does not lose sight of it.

11. Too Much Damage

by

Sean Murray

The Set-up

'Philly's coming over from Kilkenny in a couple of days,' my brother said, as he sipped on his pint.

'He's flying in on Ryan Air and has managed to get two tickets on "Sleazy Jet" for "The Damage". All the flights are fully booked though, he's been ringing around for ages and couldn't get a flight for three, it's the Tulip season and all the flights are rammed. If you can get out there yourself come along. Should be a good craic, Phil's dying to get his end away and we can have a good toke as well, Sleazy's leaving Luton at eight o'clock Thursday morning, see what you can do.'

'Nice one,' I said, 'I'll be there.'

The gauntlet had been laid down. I had five days to make the connection, I've got the cash, passport's in order and the crops are looking good. I'm up for the challenge, but I've gotta work fast.

I finished my pint of Guinness, left The Patch and jumped into the Beamer. After rolling a joint for the journey, I turned the key in the ignition and the engine's six cylinders roared into life. With a flick from the Zippo I lit the joint, after a few pulls of Northern Lights 5 Haze I slipped the car into gear and drove away. First stop: Going Places.

Game on!

Finding a space in Hemel's car park was unusually easy. 'The Gods must be with me,' I thought, as I polished off the last of the Northern Lights 5 Haze. Getting out of the car I locked the door and fastened my Parka against the wind.

I entered Going Places five minutes later and was greeted by a leggy travel agent.

'Can I help you, sir?' she said, smiling.

I relayed my requirements to her but had little success.

'There's not much here,' she said. 'I think it's the Tulip season.'

'I know,' I said.

Going Places had only three flights available, all at unreasonable times and all very expensive. I'd have to try something else. Going Places! Going Nowhere! I thought to myself, as I entered the bustle of the High Street. Next stop: Thomas Cook. If it was good enough for Phileas Fogg, it was surely good enough for me. Around the world in eighty days they could manage, but return flights to Holland at the height of Tulip mania, no chance. The grail was appearing elusive.

I tried Hemel's third and final travel agents, again with no joy. My quarry was eluding me and the travel agents were a no go it seemed. I decided to return to the Beamer and roll another joint; I was in need of some inspiration and had to plan my next move.

As I sat in the car toking, I pressed play on the stereo. The sweet smell of Marijuana swept through the car and the hypnotic sounds of Jazzanova soothed my mind and helped my meditation. Travel agents were out, what should I do next? I could phone more travel agents further afield, however I was sceptical of the results, I could surf the net, but surely there was something else.

I decided to phone the airlines direct. Next stop base camp, get out the Mellow Pages and hit the phones. One phone call to KLM Airlines was all I needed, they had the perfect flight: leaving Gatwick at 8.30 and returning Monday at 18.00 hrs Dutch time, all for £85. As I replaced the receiver I felt somewhat pleased with my performance. My counsel had advised me that there were no flights to be had, and after receiving little joy from the usual channels I had scored a flight in a few hours. £10 cheaper than my brother's on Dutch national airlines and departing from Gatwick, which everyone knows is far more rock & roll than Luton.

I lit up a bong to celebrate. After chillin' for half an hour, I contemplated what I needed for the forthcoming expedition. I decided to go upstairs and look at the garden. Priority number one. The crop was looking fine, it had been growing for two weeks and the plants were truly magnificent. Eighteen inches already, twelve years growing-experience had taught me much. This was going to be the best harvest ever, I was certainly the finest gardener in the whole kingdom. I thought back to my first guerrilla crop all those years ago in my father's shed, how far I had come. I'd start the flowering process just before leaving for Amsterdam and would be harvesting in little over a month.

Life was sweet!

I returned to The Patch in order to relay my good news, I saw my brother, drank several pints and had several toots of coka. I then returned home for bongs before bedtime, feeling very contented.

The next few days ticked over nicely. Cash was collected on time, clothes were returned from my mother's, cleaned and ironed to the usual high standard. I also finished the illustration I'd been working on over the previous couple of weeks.

Due to another heavy night before, Wednesday started fairly late. The day was spent ensuring the crop would survive its period of neglect. Fans were checked, timer switches were set to twelve hours flowering, reservoir was filled and nutrients changed and calibrated. A slightly weak solution would be in order to compensate for the inevitable evaporation that would occur while I was away. Finally, hydroponic tables were flushed, several times to ensure optimum running and correct drainage. The last thing I wanted was to return home to a dead crop and a flooded house.

The garden was running nicely and I was confident that it would be fine while I was away. Next I had to score some 'big nose' for the trip. Dutch street coke is shite, and I would have to go prepared. I'd arranged to meet Turkish in The Leinster at 6.30 to score the chassel. I'd have to keep the pleasantries to a minimum however, in order to get back and do my packing. Unfortunately quick missions and seeing Turkish didn't usually go together. That evening was to be no exception. Many pints and a head full of Columbia later I finally got into bed at around 2 a.m., bags still unpacked. I'd set the timer on my stereo to wake me at 6.30 the following morning, my lift was to be arriving at 7.

Too Much Damage!

6.30 a.m.: the stereo kicked into action, I leapt out of bed, showered, packed my bags and filled my hip flask with Remy Martin. I took a gram of weed along for the journey to the airport, stashed the coke, then horsed down a bong of NL5. The doorbell rang as I blew the smoke from my lungs, I turned off the stereo, grabbed my bags and left for Freetown.

Arriving at Amsterdam Central at 11.30, I was in good time to meet my brother and cousin at the Grasshopper at twelve o'clock, and proceed with the first hardcore smoking session of the weekend. Several high-grade Dutch joints later we made our way to the Hotel Mevlana as was the tradition, it had been home for every Dutch trip since 1990 and in twelve years the place hadn't changed at all.

The weekend turned out to be just what the doctor ordered. My cousin got laid by a Dutch brass, as he had hoped. I chatted up some Dutch babes and hooked up with an old pal Wernard. Wernard was the dealer from the Greenhouse Coffee Shop, the finest smoking establishment in the whole of Amsterdam. We all got stoned!

The End Game

After missing my original flight home I arrived back in Blighty fully recharged. It had been the best Dutch mission yet and there had been quite a few. However, as I pulled up outside my cribb my heart stopped. I looked over at the front door as it swung in the wind.

'I fucking know what's happened here!' I exclaimed, as the car parked. 'SHIT!' I entered my violated house and within a few seconds I could feel the long arm of the law upon my shoulder, they had been lying in wait outside, in an unmarked car. In my haste to leave the previous Thursday I had neglected to disarm the alarm function on my stereo and for the following four days music had been blasting the neighbours and they had called the police. The police had resisted the temptation to intercede for the first few days, but kicked the door in, it turned out, only thirty minutes before I had returned home. Inside they found a promotion waiting for them and with no work involved. If I had arrived home on the previous flight as planned, it never would have happened. I had been busted.

GAME OVER!!!

Glossary

Beamer: Car, BMW
Big Nose, Coka, Chassel: Cocaine
Damage: Amsterdam
Mellow Pages: Yellow Pages
Northern Lights 5 Haze: Extremely Potent Marijuana Hybrid

12. There is Another Way

by

H. B.

I was eight years old when I had my first drink. I stole two beers from the fridge for my best mate and myself. She took one sip and said it was disgusting. I drank both mine and hers. That's pretty much how it continued. She's still my best mate twenty-seven years later. She's married with two kids, good career, very healthy. Unfortunately that's not my story.

I knew I had a problem from a young age. When I was fifteen I wrote in my diary: 'I think I may be an alcoholic, I'm craving a drink even though I'm hung over.' I drank differently to everyone else. I couldn't tell you what would happen if I got drunk, but I knew it would be pretty bad. By the time I scraped into University, the doctor had me on antibuse and valium. He told me to only drink two drinks at a time or I'd be violently ill. So I dutifully drank two drinks at a time. Eventually, I threw the antibuse away. He referred me for alcohol abuse counselling. It took place in a dingy room behind the bombed-out shell of Coventry Cathedral. She told me to keep a diary of my drinking, how much I drank and why. I discovered then that I drank for any reason or feeling going, and that quite often I would have no idea how much I drank as I'd started having serious blackouts. Once I woke up to find myself driving on the motorway doing ninety. Another time I was raped. Pretty soon I stopped going to the counsellor. My problem was that I didn't want to stop; I was having too much fun.

By then I was drinking every day to get drunk but just not getting the same effect. That's when I started doing drugs. I'd already been smoking pot since I was sixteen. Now it was on to ecstasy, acid, speed and cocaine. But not heroin. Heroin was for drug addicts and I wasn't one of those, I was just a little bit messed up and so would you be if you'd had my childhood. I'd been sexually abused as a kid and I grew up in a house full of confusion and hostility. The first thing I learned to control was my food.

I knew the calorie content of every food imaginable by the time I was nine. Then later on, the drink and the drugs, well, they just helped me feel normal, helped me fit in. But then the panic attacks and depression started.

I tried AA at this point. I was nineteen. A woman in her fifties from the East End came over to my parents' flat in Kensington where I was staying. She talked to me about her life and took me to a meeting in the city. I am sure I was the only one there under fifty. I didn't know what the fuck anyone was talking about. I still didn't really want to stop drinking, I felt sure that there must be a way out of this without having to do that. But the depression just kept getting worse.

I'd graduated, just, from University by then. I didn't know what I was going to do with my life. The doctor prescribed more pills; Prozac, this time, then when that didn't work I tried a whole lot more anti-depressants, Lustral, Effexor, MAOIs, SSRIs; you name them, I tried them. And then the painkillers: Codeine, Pethidine, anything I could get my hands on. The trips to hospital had started, my health started to give, physically now as well as mentally. My liver was damaged, I had pancreatitis. I developed pleurisy. Was told that my chances of conceiving a baby were limited. Couldn't hold down a job. Went out with some real losers. Then I started smoking heroin.

One day I woke up and realised I'd been praying to die for as long as I could remember. My life felt like I was on a runaway train, moving faster and faster through tunnels, whizzing past stations that I was desperate to get off at. I knew the only destination was certain death. And I was frightened because I didn't really want to die, I just didn't want to feel the way I did or have to listen to those voices in my head telling me what a fuck-up I was, what a mess my life had become and how no one would ever love me, how could they when I was so disgusting, so abhorrent in every way. I was twenty-six when I had a nervous breakdown. I ended up in hospital in a catatonic state, rocking myself silently in the corner of my room. I went through the dts, hallucinations, dry heaves, the sweats, horrendous panic attacks. It felt like I was being given endless little electric shocks. My body shook for months. I ended up in a treatment centre. Every time I opened my mouth I had to say, 'My name is H and I'm an alcoholic, drug addict, chemically dependent, co-dependant, anorexic, compulsive overeater.' I wanted the ground to swallow me up. I felt like my skin had been flayed and doused with vinegar. I huddled in the smoking-room cocooned in the safety of the cigarette smoke.

After four months there, I came to and decided to end it. One bottle of Jack Daniels and a few packets of pills later, and I ended up back in the hospital. How ironic, I thought, that it's my twenty-seventh birthday. How much I dreaded growing sober – even another day. But that has now become my sobriety date. I have not had another drink or drug since that day nearly nine years ago, and I honestly can't tell you why or how. All that I know is that part of me died that day. I had the whole 'near death' experience, long tunnel, bright healing light, feeling of incredible peace and love. I guess I've come to believe that a spiritual awakening occurred as I lay in that hospital that day; my soul cried out that I needed to find another way to survive and that once I had found that way I needed to learn how to celebrate life, not endure it. And I was to return to this body and spend the rest of my life dedicated to finding this other way. And through regularly attending twelve-step fellowships, and being open and willing to experience other forms of teaching, changing and healing on every level, I am indeed celebrating my life; celebrating it through my paintings, celebrating it through my beautiful four-year-old son, celebrating it through my friends, my partner and my family, and now celebrating it with you, the reader.

I have self-love and self-acceptance, maybe not all of the time, but most of the time. I don't want to hurt or destroy myself anymore, and I love my life. And I don't question why or how today, I just try to experience today in all its glory and know that it feels good to be alive and it feels good to be clean and sober.

13. Bleed Me Dry

by

H. A.

I am seventeen, but I feel older, and my Mum says you're only as old as you feel.

I hang out with the older kids, smoking cigarettes and drinking warm, sour beer in dingy, dark clubs, and they don't treat me any differently just because I'm younger. Mum treats me like I'm older, so she can go out with her boyfriend while I look after my little sister Kate who wants me to play house, but I sneak out into endless velvet nights after putting her to bed. Boys think I'm older and they think this gives them certain rights. Sometimes, in the corners of darkened clubs on nights where I'm empty of hope and there's nothing left to lose, I think that too.

I am seventeen and today I did something weird, very weird, but it felt so right. This was not the first time. Not the first time I went into the bathroom and opened the mirrored cabinet, cringing at the creak of the rusty hinges. Not the first time my fingers crept past Mum's birth control pills, searching among old crusty pallets of eye shadow and between tester bottles of cheap perfume, seeking my target. My hand rests on a pack of new razor blades. Bull's-eye. I pull them out, carefully, and release one of them from its transparent plastic sleeping place. I look at it. The blade glints a promise under the harsh single bulb in the bathroom. It is silver, and cold, and clean. This is my chosen instrument, my saviour, my release.

I roll up my sleeve to reveal skin that was once a blank canvas, soft and white and smooth like a child's. But I am not a child. I am seventeen, and this is my arm, on my body, and this is my blade and my choice. At least, I think it is. Lately it seems that the blade has chosen me, and I have a criss-cross mess of self-inflicted scars to prove it. The blade calls and I come to it, because I am empty of any other answers, and I have so many questions. I want to peel off my skin, layer by layer, and find my molten-hot core, find out what is wrong and why I'm different.

Blade meets flesh. It's quick, this release, and painless, although you probably wouldn't believe it. Then the contact. A nanosecond of savouring the moment when the fire of my flesh meets the ice of the blade, and then that's gone and I'm doing it, I'm pressing down, hard, gritting my teeth, but it's not hard enough, and then I'm swiping at my arm and feel sweet release, sweet relief. Watching the blood drain away down the plughole in a thick slash of crimson. The ball of fury and pain in my stomach drains away with this stringy red stuff drip, drip, dripping from my arm. Vacant-eyed I stare. This is what I have the power to do.

I am seventeen, and already I am the walking wounded.

*

Here is my happiest memory –

It happened almost a year ago. My friend Clare and I, down by the river in the park. We were best friends back then, but I haven't seen her since and I never will again. I made a mistake because I didn't know what she was thinking, not even what I was thinking, when I leant over and kissed her in the shade of a weeping willow. The foliage whispered overhead and dappled patches of sun played on her milk-white, milk-sweet skin. I looked at her and wanted her, which I've never felt before with the older guys who just want a quick fuck to gloat about with their friends. But she didn't pull away and our lips met, and I felt like I was melting into her, the coil of confusion and scarlet hurt which had set up home in the pit of my stomach relaxed and it was just me and her, alone, everything soft and perfect. It felt perfect. And I realised, this is what I've been scared of. This is what I wanted. This is the answer, not another razor scar burning into my flesh.

Did I say it was my happiest memory? What happened next has almost snatched that away, although I still savour that kiss. Flesh of my flesh, we were one, just for a fleeting moment.

I thought we were hidden, but the boys saw us. The kind of boys you avoid, who have a gang at school. They were there all along, plain as day, but not to me, lost in my world of Clare. I had forgotten the outside world until a rock hit the surface of the river, splashing Clare and me with water that burned. I turned and saw them, staring as though hypnotised, with sneers scarring their faces and crumpled cans of lager in their fists.

'Oi! Lesbos!' One of them with a pockmarked face yelled. 'Can't yer get a bloke?'

'Maybe they just haven't had a real one! Hear that, dykes? All you need is a real man!'

'She's that fucking weirdo from our school. Oi bitch, want some of this?' And with that, Pock-Face unzipped his flies and released his flaccid cock, looking proud of himself, wiggling it in my direction.

My stomach dropped and my world spun around me. A few seconds ago I was floating on the calm lake of happiness, but they had thrown me into an ocean roaring with the poison promise of what I was, what I was to become, what they would make me become once the rumour got around school.

And then something worse. Clare was gone, no longer by my side. I looked and there was nothing but empty space where she had been, and her kiss evaporating too quickly from my lips. Frantically I searched the riverbank for her, broke through the undergrowth with branches scratching at my face, calling her name, but only silence answered.

'Even yer girlfriend don't wanna fuck you no more!'

I hated them, and they hated me, but at that moment all I wanted was to find Clare. I thought I caught a glimpse of her running across the bridge towards the nice part of town, where she lived. She lived with her family and went to the Catholic girls' school on the other side of town to our Comprehensive.

I ran after her. In her I thought I had found something real, something to fill the emptiness, something to replace all the hurt I'd felt and all the guilt because I knew I was different, but I didn't want to be different, not any more. I would have run across the world for her, danced along the oceans because I had known her since forever and been in love with her for longer. I would have run until my feet wore down to the bone if I'd thought I could catch her.

But I realised I couldn't. Even if I caught up with her, what would she want to do with me? She was a Catholic. She was rich. She was popular, and pretty, and clever. She would go far and she would get there without me. The truth is, she had too much to risk. I was just an experiment gone horribly wrong. Lucky for her, they hadn't seen her face properly. Mine sheltered it.

But they did see my face, and now they are running after me seeking revenge. I ran home, all the way, breathless and red-faced and sweating, an anger and fear which I couldn't express. Tears welled in my eyes. I had lost her, and I knew it would be the last time I saw her. I'm still running and trying to find a quick fix. Her love could have fixed me, but when I got home and locked myself shaking and panting in the bathroom, away from Mum's difficult questions and the four-walled cell of my bedroom, Clare was nowhere to be found.

But the razorblades were.

*

They were there then, when I was sweet sixteen and scared but in love, a love thick enough and deep enough to fill in the empty spaces in my heart.

Now that's gone and I'm empty and void of all feeling except the pain that Clare left behind when she ran away.

And they are there now, those sweet silver promises like a vampire's kiss on my skin. At first it was controlled. I remember the first time, I was shaving the dark fuzz off my legs in the bath with sad acoustic music dripping lovelorn declarations from my tinny stereo, and I was sad, so sad, just thinking about Clare and about school and about how I would never, ever fit in. And all of a sudden I was overcome with a rage at myself, a burning flame of anger and hatred at what I had allowed myself to become. A quick flick of the wrist was all it took. Then I lay there in a lukewarm bath with a crimson trickle crawling down my ankle, and only the cooling embers of my anger were left. I thought I had found the answer.

I am different. Queer. Weird. I am strange and people don't like strangeness, they like familiarity and people who strive for acceptance, which I have long stopped attempting to do. They don't like that they can't categorise me. Even my older friends are starting to realise it now. I wonder how long it will take before I fade away completely. And yet I cannot leave. My life, miserable and pathetic as it is, is here, in the dog-shit alleys of our dingy city, in the alcohol-blurred Saturday nights under neon loneliness, in the broken family unit my mother tries to glue back together every so often. I cannot run away because wherever I run, I end up running into myself.

*

I decide to stop going to school, so sick am I of the disgusted stares and violent shoves against my locker, of the cool kids shouting insults and everyone avoiding me in case they catch it, catch not just Queerness, but the unidentifiable disease, the loneliness which makes me so strange.

Mum works in the hospital, looking after sick and dying people to pay for our terraced house near the city centre, to keep the temperamental boiler from packing in for good, to keep food in the cupboards even though I barely touch it now. Another day brings another low. They say you have to hit rock bottom to truly recover, but I'm still free-falling through endless layers of pain waiting to land.

Before Mum leaves I get dressed for school, get Kate dressed, feed her and drink a cup of coffee and then take her to school. I loiter there for a while until she's been subsumed into her crowds of cute friends, all sweet and pure and innocent of this depression that's eating me up inside. I wish I could go back to childhood, back to endless balmy summer days. I feel like nuclear winter.

Then I turn back and retrace my steps. Back through rush hour traffic and everyone going somewhere, everyone with something to do. Not me. I have dropped out of this life. But I do have something waiting for me at home. I try to look at the fading autumn glow of the city, which people say is beautiful – at the rich reds and browns and pale blue sky fading to white beyond the skyline, but all I see are silver promises, icy blades, the release which awaits me.

So here I lie, in stained crumpled sheets sprinkled with stray brown tobacco strands, with my instruments lined up. I don't bother to sterilise the blades, I figure if I die I die, I feel like the undead anyway, these thin layers of clothing barely concealing a body shrinking fast and littered with scar upon scar upon scar. My body is a battleground and every day I add a new injury. My body, a map of previous pain. Point to a scar and like a tour guide I can tell you its origin, its history, all you want to know and a few things you don't. But although the blood comes loyally slithering from my veins, inside me every capillary is a knot too complex to untie. My body is an aneurysm.

I feel old and tiny, shrinking away from everyday life in my cold empty bed. Outside is golden autumn, but the sunlight dripping onto my carpet in pools of treacle does nothing to pierce the fog in my head. The day is stubborn, its shades ebb and flow, but I am not a part of its weak tide. Such a surprise to realise that whatever you do or don't do, still the tide turns, still the white day turns to navy dusk, whether you crawl out of bed or not. The selfish day which waits for no man. The insistent day which cannot be wished away.

I want my self back. I am a bloody mess and I thought I could control it but it is controlling me. Something goes wrong and I reach for the blade. Someone looks at me the wrong way and I reach for the blade. I just feel like escaping myself for a while, and I reach for the blade. It delivers, in spades of enveloping warm release. But it seems to be controlling me, here, now, lying under blankets wishing the day away with a piece of metal for company.

I'm sick … physically and mentally torn asunder. Self-mutilation is a common-sense act designated to bringing the outer body down to the level of pain and degradation felt by the mental self. My scars throb scarlet beneath my clothes, weeping red tears. I am the walking wounded and I don't know why I hurt but it's in my stomach's pit and behind my eyes, swelling up in my mind.

Eventually, I have cut so much that there is nothing but blood and scars all up my arms. My skin is stained with my guilty secret. The evidence is branded into my flesh. I feel myself drifting into sleep, and I know my Mum will be home soon and I know she will be mad and upset and hysterical, but maybe that is what I need now. Not the silver kiss of metal but the real, alive kiss of human love. She will save me.

This is my cry for help, my admission of guilt and my twelve-step plan all in one. I don't want this to be me any longer. I am a slave to the blade. I want recovery. I look in the mirror and all I see is a scarlet wound in place of my reflection.

I am seventeen. Throw me a lifeline.

14. The Grandson and the Daughter

by

Ray Tollady

Bill drove a coach and four, a late nineteenth-century horse-drawn taxi; he earned good money all paid in cash. The coins were stored in a large demy jar on the mantelshelf over the cooking-range in the tiny Victorian two-bedroom terraced house, a rented family home in the back streets of Birmingham. Bill was married to a beautiful woman and they had nine children, eight survived childbirth but three were killed in the Great War. The family were exceedingly poor for despite his earnings Bill was an alcoholic and drank all day from the whisky bottle beneath the seat, and he drank all night at the corner public house. Bill drank the demy jar empty of its silver. He was a kind man when sober but violent when drunk, he was insanely jealous and possessive of his beautiful wife and often beat her violently when his distorted mind believed she had been flirting with the other men.

Bill's youngest daughter left home at the age of sixteen for she could not cope with the unhappiness.

The daughter married and had two children, the youngest, a son, was born in the image of Bill, a grandson born as a reincarnation of his grandfather and the grandson married a beautiful woman, they had two children and the grandson was a drunk, an alcoholic who was insanely jealous and possessive. Whilst not physically violent to his wife he was emotionally and verbally abusive and his youngest daughter left home when she was seventeen for she could not cope with the unhappiness.

The grandson's slide to dependence on alcohol was slow and painful, and brought much grief to his family. In the beginning he drank only in the late evenings when the emotional turmoil crept surreptitiously into the corners of his mind. During the day he coped with the normal processes of business and family life, but in the evenings he needed alcohol to sedate his insecurity and his fears for the future. Alcohol brought the relief he craved, but his illness was progressive and his reliance on the chemical increased, and day by day the illness grew and by middle-age he was drinking in the daylight hours before leaving his work. He drank in secret and in isolation and lied to his family, and the blackouts began and his eyes grew grey and bloated and he passed the moment of choice – for now he had to drink and, although he knew that he was addicted, it made no difference. He was destined to live for years in deep denial and in the clutches of alcohol. His family lived the pain. They were subjects of his irrational behaviour, his anger and his frustration and it was unrelenting.

Society had changed in the years since grandfather Bill had died, women had fought for emancipation, and the wife and children of the grandson found the courage to leave him and to take their rightful share of the family estate, for the family had found education and a profession, and were living the life of the middle-classes.

He sat alone in the hallway of his small terraced home, the phone was disconnected and he hid the Vodka bottle in the cupboard below the stairs; it was noon on a bleak Saturday, he was already drunk and he knew his life was finished. At the age of fifty-five the grandson was alone, his business was failing, he had little money and the cost of his drinking exceeded his ability to earn. He needed the alcohol more than he needed his departed family and he was depressed and physically debilitated. Subconsciously

he knew of the pain and suffering he had brought to his loved ones and he wished to find the courage to end his life quickly to evade the promise of the misery that the remainder of his life held. He woke each day in tears of regret and remorse, of guilt and shame. He shook and heaved, sweated and ached and swore he would never drink again. He had little memory of the previous day, of whom he had insulted or abused, but he knew that he often offended or abused someone somewhere. But by midday the monster had returned, deep in his body, the urge for alcohol had returned and he had no power to resist. His fading mind knew it was wrong, knew it was self-destructive but he had no choice, he had to do it, he had to drink the poison, and as he unscrewed the cap of the Vodka bottle a great joy of relief swept over him and the first taste of the clear spirit brought contentment, he was fine, he could cope and, for a short time, he could be happy.

Alcoholism is an insidious obsession and he had inherited the illness from his grandfather, just as his grandfather had inherited the disease from his forefathers and, like his forefathers, he knew the drink would kill him, a slow, painful suicide he had no power to prevent.

He craved help, begged for help and prayed for the wisdom he lacked. He was told that he first had to find the courage to accept humiliation and shame and to beg for the knowledge of those who had recovered from the same terrible illness. He entered the rooms of these people in fear and trepidation. And in one moment, in an instant of his existence, a miracle took place and he found the courage. In that moment he accepted that he was an alcoholic, that he was powerless over alcohol, he was addicted to and obsessed by this chemical substance and he felt the humiliation and shame, and in that moment the denial was taken from him and he became willing to lust for sobriety. He does not know how or why this revelation appeared and how or why his addled brain came to this simple but miraculous conclusion, but it happened.

It was a painful process. For him the physical withdrawals passed quickly, but the mental turmoil lasted for many years as he learnt to live without the crutch of alcohol. For him the drinking was easy, he had inherited his grandfather's ability to absorb large quantities of alcohol. Coping with a life of sobriety was more painful. He had hidden from his emotions in the shroud of an alcoholic haze and was beset with resentments, frustrations and anger. He had used the drink to cope with his feelings of inadequacy and low self-esteem. He had been too proud to cope with embarrassment or failure and he could not find the love of others for he did not know how to love himself. But in life each person is given a second chance if they can find the courage and wisdom to change, and he found the courage, and with the help of his recovering alcoholic friends he boarded a wheel of recovery, and he fell in love.

*

She smelt the blood and felt it sliding down her face, curling under her chin and she eventually noticed the stain appear as it dripped onto her blouse. She dropped the scissors and wondered how many times she had stabbed her own face, but it did not matter for the poison was being let out, the badness within was draining away, she knew it would return, that she would need alcohol again, but at that moment the daughter was content and she settled to doze. The car was parked on a verge, daylight had faded and she did not hear the other car arrive nor her car door being opened.

She lay on her own bed and allowed the hands to wipe the wounds, and she could not understand why they did not realise that she had to do it. They would take her to a clinic for the disturbed, she would be locked in and watched and that was the way it should be for she deserved it. They would tell her to stop doing it, to stop the drinking and stop the harming, that her children loved her and she would pretend she was cured and they would send her home, but it would make no difference for she had no choice, the misery would return and it would start again, she would climb aboard the helter-skelter and be unable to prevent the slide to insanity. She knew she was insane, normal people do not drink as she drinks nor have need to draw their own blood, and maybe one day all of the badness will drain from her and the shame will die as she dies. It's the secret. She needed to keep it secret. She feels her family's love and she laboured at their birth, but she now sees the fear that has entered their lives, it pours from their eyes. But she does not want them to see her misery, so she tries to keep it a secret but it does not work and she knows it causes them more pain, it is a circle of destruction and she at the centre, but she has no choice, she has to do it.

She pushed her bicycle along the High Street, bottles of alcohol nestling in the front basket, and the grandson sees the fear in her eyes and he understands, for his eyes have looked upon the same world and his heart has grieved. She would rush to the hotel bar wearing her mask of normality and she raced through life avoiding all contact and intimacy, passing as a stranger, waving from the window as reality slipped by, for she had gorged on emptiness and her skin had breathed the pallor of dismay and he cried for her.

The grandson collected her the next evening and she was full of alcoholic courage and she bravely laughed the laughter known only to those beset with fear. Very soon the courage had left her and the laughter had left her and she was filled with the fear, but he would not concede and he took her to the place and she sat in misery and she cried. They met regularly, three or four evenings each week with the friends, but she never spoke. He talked incessantly but she did not hear for the pain remained and the hopelessness remained. The immense physical effort to exist had exhausted her and then one day she laughed and she felt brave and, though naked and unprepared, she began to fight the battle for life. She tried and she suffered; she shook and began to vomit away the poison, perspiration seeped from her every pore, her head ached and her breathing seemed to cease. She lay for hours curled in the womb of her sofa in tears of despair and yet, despite the pain, each night she was ready to go with him. Days stretched to weeks and slowly, very slowly the hurting began to ease.

She is sensitive and fragile but he hopes that she will continue to recover. That one day the frustration, anger and despair will leave and she will understand that the guilt and shame she carries belongs elsewhere. She will see that she carries the guilt and shame of her parents for they needed to be seen as the perfect parents of the perfect daughter and she is still not able to cope with this heavy burden. The grandson prays that one day the feelings of despondency will fade and the daughter will discover the childhood she lost. She will come to believe her soul is able to give joy to the hearts of others.

The grandson and the daughter know that yesterday is but a history that cannot be changed and tomorrow is a mystery that cannot be foreseen but today, this day, this wonderful day the grandson and the daughter are thankful to love and to be loved by each other and they are grateful to have been given the gift of a new life.

15. Hypochondria One

by

David Schaal

It's eating away inside me. I think it started in my bowels. Not surprising that such a bilious, contemptible cur like myself should be infected.

The doctors tell me it's nothing. 'Relax,' they say, 'it's your anxiety speaking.' But I know different. I know it's the cancer. I can feel the tumours spreading. The cells in my body rapidly reproducing and forming a black mass. I know the dark disease from within wants me dead.

My cancer speaks to me. It is very lucid and precise. It says: 'Hello, dead guy. I'm ploughing a course through your insides. I want to violate every part of you.' I don't answer back. What's the point? Cancer doesn't listen.

I just lay there quaking. I can feel it sniffing my fear like a dog. It feeds on it. If I try to take my fear away it gets angry: 'Don't be bold with me, you motherless fuck! You're dying and you know it.'

It has a vendetta against me. Against my family. It's trying to pick us off one by one. And it comes for me at night. When I'm alone. Just before I sleep. I can hear its sarcasm. 'Goodnight,' it says, 'sleep tight. Don't let the sarcomas bite.'

The doctors grin like Cheshire cats. They are adjectival with me. I hear familiar words like: fear, anxiety, worry, stress and bereavement. Then one spectacled quack slips in a new word: 'addiction.'

I recoil like a spring. A knot of fear grips me. My insides tense. I mumble and murmur. I try to distract and deflect. He's looking me straight in the eye. I whimper: 'I need an X-ray and a sigmoidoscopy.' A little knowledge is a dangerous thing.

But I don't need an X-ray because his eyes see right through me. I feel them burning, boring into my core. They torch their way through to my centre and out the other side. I am transparent. Empty. His gaze burns through the hole in my soul. He knows the only cancer they will find is in my mind.

In the knowledge of this, relief floods through me. It was just another one of my voices. It wasn't real. For the third time this week I skip out of the surgery. This last one wasn't too bad. Maybe he's not a quack after all. He has insight. He's convinced me. I'm not dying! My heart skips with excitement. It flutters.

Funny that. It's been fluttering a lot lately. Whenever I exercise or get excited. Extra heart beat they told me. But I *know* it's not. I check my pulse: 18 beats every 15 seconds. Hmmm strange. I can feel something eating away at my aortic valve. It wasn't cancer at all. It was heart disease all along …

16. Hypochondria Two

by

David Schaal

Tick, tick, tock. Tick, tick, tock. Tick, tick, tock. My heart beats steady in rhythm to the clock. I check for any signs of labouring or stress. All seems normal and regular. The early morning surge that roused me from my slumber has subsided. Tick, tick, tock. The heart beats in rhythm to the clock. Tick, tick, tock.

Mornings are always the worst. I often wake from my sleep with a start. Heart pulsing strong, bedding wet from my tortured night sweats. Head full of visions and voices, I am like a walking film montage of disjointed thoughts and sensations. It's always my mother's shrill voice: 'Michael? Michael?! It's eight o'clock!' A sort of sensational recall from my school days.

I struggle to the bathroom. Take a look in the mirror and see a stranger staring back at me. I smile. Dead eyes gaze fixedly. Who are you? I do not recognise that listless grey pallor that looks blankly at me. The face has become jowly and reddened. Clear and milky skin has given way to broken blood vessels. The eyes are bloodshot red. A coughing fit ensues. The voices take me back to my childhood once more. This time it's my sister. I am seventeen and staring at myself in the mirror.

'You're a narcissist.'

'What's that?'

'A story of a boy who stared at his reflection in water and fell in love with himself.'

'I'm not the only one who is in love with my reflection!' I counter.

'Yeah well, he fell in and drowned.'

'Girls drown in my good looks.'

'Don't make me puke!'

'Don't watch me then!'

'Get out. I need the bathroom.'

'Bugger off.'

'Hurry up, yellow teeth! You'll be fine as long as you don't smile.' She is gone in a cruel expose of my warts and all.

My coughing fit subsides. Must my days always begin thus? I bare my teeth like a Rottweiler. My sister's prophecy is true. My teeth are yellow, stained by cigarettes and tea. I pick up the worn toothbrush and frenetically clean my teeth. I spit out blood into the basin. Shit! Need more vitamin C. Need to stop smoking as my gums are receding. The dentist called them 'pockets'. I check my neck for my jugular vein pulse. It seems very fast still. The doorbell rings. The pulse rate jumps and goes off the Richter scale! Panic, fear and dread in equal measures. Is that my car already? Too bloody early again. I open the door. A fat, sweaty driver stands on my doorstep. I look back at him in disgust.

'Are you Michael?' he enquires.

'Yes.' I half smile, aware of my dental shortcomings. 'Are you early?' I retort.

'Only about ten minutes. I was hoping to beat the traffic.'

A knot of fear grips my insides. Have I messed up again? 'Won't be a minute.' The fat man waddles back to his car, disappointed at my indolence. 'Fuck you,' I mutter under my breath as he wobbles away. 'You have no idea what I'm going through.'

I go back to the bathroom. Ten minutes to be out the door. No time to indulge my voices. A rush of adrenaline kicks in. I feel my heart add a beat. Ouch! The old familiar panic kicks in. As the giant in David Lynch's *Twin Peaks* warned: 'It is happening again!' I run a bath trying to stay calm. One of my voices makes a very useful comment: 'You fucking idiot. Not only did you drink too much last night, you got up too late. You are going to cock it up today that's for sure! I wouldn't like to be you on set today.' I ignore it and grab a hasty bath. Once my clothes are off I realise that I am challenging my fat driver in the girth stakes. My swollen stomach makes it difficult to negotiate getting in and out of the bath. I am panting and wheezing like an old cart horse. My heart lurches again as I strain to bend over and pull up my trousers. I begin to wonder who the voice belongs to. Then I realise: it's me. The special critical inner voice that reserves itself for my weakest moments, my lowest ebb. It takes a final swipe: 'You are fatter than Buddha!'

I sit in the car staring at the driver's pockmarked neck. Angry blemishes rage on his skin. His greying, black hair a chaotic mess. He is puffy and sweaty and way out of shape. 'Just like looking in the mirror, isn't it?' my voice says, helpfully. The fat driver blathers on moronically. He tries to engage me in vacuous conversation but I answer monosyllabically. His attempts to draw me on my salary anger me, and I go sullenly silent. All I am concentrating on is my heart. Once again it takes an extra beat that reverberates through me. 'Christ, that was a sharp one. Must be something to do with your arteries.' My voice knows this is familiar territory. It triggers an instant image of my entire artery network clogging up. I imagine Hieronymous Bosch depicting the tube system in London: all black and dangerous, populated by grotesque gargoyles spewing a black tarlike substance from their entrails. The film starts to roll in my head again. I am being pursued by demons, hunting me down, trying to violate my body and mind in pursuit of my soul.

Finally, we arrive at the location. I am in no mood to be shooting a commercial. I am greeted warmly by the First Assistant Director, a woman I worked with before on a previous project. She is gripping my hand and commenting on how well I look. She tells me I have lost weight since the last time we worked together. 'Jesus Christ. What must you have looked like then?' my voice chimes in, supportively. She must be lying I reply to myself. These professional schmoozers are no use to me in my frame of mind. I need some real time, love and affection. From somebody I can trust. My mind digresses to Julia, my ex-girlfriend. God, how I've missed her. She was such a soothing influence on me in times like this. The film plays on. We have moved on from horror to romance. How Julia used to tell me how much she loved me. How she would stroke my arms and gaze into my eyes full of love. 'Bollocks!' interjects my voice, cutting the film short like a spliced negative. 'She thought you were a lazy, fat, good-for-nothing slob who snored like a warthog.' Did she? Yes. That's true. That was the truth. But she was willing to throw her lot in with me. To offer me the warm hand of bondage, the familiar cruelty of coupledom. She may not have liked me much, but she loved me ...

The First AD ushers me to my dressing-room and tells me that we are a while away from starting yet.

'Get yourself some breakfast,' she says. The emotional recall has upset me. 'Are you ok?' she kindly enquires. I see her mentally revising her initial assessment of me. Her eyes give away concern.

'I'm fine. I have a bit of a stomach problem,' I tell her. This is true. I was diagnosed a while ago with a hiatus hernia. These ectopic heartbeats I have been experiencing could well be linked to the hernia inside me. If it's not my arteries closing up then it is my stomach wreaking havoc as it disappears up my oesophagus. The film kicks in again. We have moved from romance to documentary. I see a vivid picture of my insides, my critical voice provides the commentary. It is like an old BBC newsreel.

'Your stomach valve separating your stomach and your oesophagus are weak because you are such a fat bastard.' The film zooms in on the weak valve. I see it bending and straining under assault from the microscopic fatty deposits which in my mind's eye are like little lumps of porridge. 'These fatty deposits are eventually absorbed by your blood stream and over a long period of time clog up your arteries causing restriction of the blood flow to and from your heart, this is called angina.'

The AD short-circuits the movie. 'Maybe you need a good old fry-up to sort that out!' She gives me a knowing wink. I take her advice and tuck into my usual full English breakfast. I muse over how I got myself into this state. Last night was weird. I met up with Roger in the pub for a 'quickie'. I was euphoric about filming today as this particular commercial is big bucks. I only intended on having one drink, but then self-congratulation took over. I pontificated about my life and career, and seven pints and a kebab later I had passed out in demonic slumber.

I felt worse after eating. I was starting to sweat freely and my stomach seemed to be expanding by the second. As I walked from the dining-car to my mobile dressing-room a sudden spasm in my chest sent me into panic overdrive. I stood rooted to the spot. The AD spotted my fear and came quickly over.

'Are you OK?'

'I've got pains in my chest.'

'Right. I'm going to get you to hospital.' She made an instant call on her mobile and a car whisked round to run me to a nearby hospital.

'What about filming?' I tried to dissuade myself from getting in the car.
'Don't you worry about anything here. Your health is more important.'
'If I'm OK I'll come back.'

She nodded at me, doubtfully. 'I'll ring the producers and tell them.'

In the car on the way to hospital my inner voice took the gloves off.
'You really have fucked it up this time. You will never get employed again.
There is nothing fucking wrong with you. You are going to lose a lot of
money because you're a fucking hypochondriac!'

My internal dialogue raged at my voice. 'You told me I had angina. It's
your fault!'

'If you hadn't got pissed last night none of this would have happened.
You're an unprofessional piss-head oaf!' I sent my voice to Coventry for
the rest of the journey, my anger forcing stony silence between us. As I got
out of the car the fat driver came round to assist me. I felt ashamed of
myself for my earlier attitude towards him as I saw genuine concern on his
face. My voice rained in one more low blow: 'Better let him help you out
since you're having a heart attack.' I could hear it laughing as I walked
effortlessly into the accident and emergency department.

They shaved my chest and rigged me up to an electrocardiogram
machine. Disgusted with myself, I was now completely calm as I realised
the scale of the impact my fear was beginning to have on my life. This was
my 20th ECG in a year. All caused by the same cycle of drinking, fear and
panic. The doctor came in and gave me a clean bill of health.

The voice was about to start up again: 'There goes six months' income
…' But I short-circuited it. I had to save my job. I rang the lovely AD and
she informed me to go home and rest as a replacement actor had been sent
for. My eyes welled up.

'But I'm OK,' I blubbered. 'They said I'm fine.'

Pause on the other end. 'OK, Michael, let me ring the producer.'

The producer rang me back a few minutes later. 'Hello, Michael. Gosh
what a morning for you. How are you?'

I knew I had to talk my way out of the smelly stuff. 'I am absolutely fine.
I have a very minor stomach problem which can give me sensations in my
chest, but it is nothing to do with my heart.'

'You know we were just about to send for a replacement actor.'

'Don't bother, I'm fine,' I said, curtly.

'You're not going to keel over on us, are you?'

'No. It's absolutely nothing. I am fine.' The longest two-second silence of my life ensued.

'OK, Michael. You were our first choice and we really want you to do it. If you get a letter of release from the doctor, saying you are OK to work, then you can come back.'

'Cancel the other actor. I already have the letter,' I lied.

'Oh, that's great news. See you soon, then. The director said all along you are his first choice. I think we need to be gentle with you today.'

The phone clicked off. I sent the fat driver in to do my dirty work and get a letter from the doctor. He eagerly obliged feeling a growing sense of my favour towards him. He secured the letter and all the way back to set I rewarded him with acting stories and who I'd worked with. But I still never talked to the nosy git about money.

Once on set a sublime day ensued. My voice kept largely quiet as I went about my work with a confidence and lightness of touch that I had rarely demonstrated and that was born out of sheer relief. The result was some of the best work I have done. I even joked about keeling over on the job, and all the people involved in the commercial back-patted and glad-handed me, telling me how I was always their first choice. When I got home, the euphoria subsided and I was suddenly filled with a terror about how close I'd come to losing a lucrative and fun-filled job. In fact, the emotions were so intense that I rang Roger and met him for a 'quickie' in the pub.

17. Night Fishing

by

P. C.

First of all I felt it, right through my body: the disturbance. I knew he was terribly disturbed and dangerous. Then I looked at him and his eyes were glinty like a bad dog's. His face was damp. He kept sighing. Without even speaking he went into the bathroom and started washing his sweaters. He washed them violently, still with a great deal of sighing. The panic was rising, as obvious as the steam.

I tried to talk to him, to say, 'What's wrong?'

He walked out as though he was going to murder someone. He looked like a Frankenstein experiment.

So I talked to his brother, who said yes, he was taking a lot of dope and it obviously didn't suit him. That was a lot from someone who only saw the good in everything.

A girlfriend had thrown him out and he was living half the time in cardboard city. I didn't believe it. I had to wait a good safe while before I could believe it. I tried to find him and he showed up suddenly with a street girl. He said they were closing cardboard city and asked for money. He turned a pair of alien eyes on me, then took out all the plugs from the electric sockets. The girl had seen all this before and got up and left. And then he looked terrible, and I could see we were talking about something other than cardboard city.

The worst part was knowing where he was heading and not being able to do one thing about it. The boy I loved had disappeared for ever, and there was some deranged stranger in his place. Of course I knew it was coming. You couldn't take that much dope and drink and be so disturbed without courting a tragedy. I tried to stop him. I can truly say I did everything in my power to make him give up. I tried to get him to see doctors. I did get him into a clinic – he stayed two hours. He couldn't even admit how badly wrong things were in his mind. I tried to get him to go to his priest. No, I could not do one thing to stop what happened. During that time I learned you can't take a person's free will away even if they're on the highway to hell. I also learned that a mother will try to save her child by drawing the illness into herself, taking it on, so allowing him the chance to be well. For a while I thought the horror of it had turned my body against itself. I didn't see how my body could hold out.

Then he was finally hospitalised. The patients were in a bad state, yet he, who was so fastidious, even arrogant, learned compassion in that place. Then he wanted to get out. He rang me in panic after he'd been in a month: 'Mum, this is a mental hospital. I'll go mad if I stay here.' No amount of persuasion from the staff changed his mind, and by the law of the land he was now free. Dr O'Connor solved it. 'Come out for a trial weekend. See how you feel. Make sure you can handle it,' he said.

We all gathered round – his friends, mine – and tried to make it work for him. Now he seemed so sweet, piteous and broken – it did just about break my heart. The anti-psychotic drugs made him shake and inflamed his nerves to such a degree he said it was unbearable.

We took him on to Hampstead Heath and his friends supported him, helped him walk. That was the worst moment of all, seeing him helpless and ruined against the beauty of the summer evening. He could move only slowly, shakily, and his face was unrecognisable. He was a completely different person. Not my child. And he looked so full of suffering and so pathetic I couldn't bear it, and I walked ahead on my own towards the ponds and the tears started fast down my face. It was the first time I'd really cried. Crying seemed to have had no place in all this. I hated life for what it had done to my child. And I think it was because he was now so sweet and suffering so much, and trying his best to hide it, that my heart did actually break, and the pain I felt during all those months burst like a diseased appendix. I could do nothing to help him, only observe and suffer. I didn't trust life. I ran to the railway bridge, and for the first time I knew how I would die. I had to terminate myself because I could not take the next moment. What stopped me? A mere flash of thought: what if it doesn't end and I go on in some sort of consciousness? And by my act I've added to the present chaos. What if I suffered even more? Perhaps I wouldn't escape into oblivion. Like a policeman inside my mind, the thought insisted on respectful consideration. Leaping out was like taking a very high dive. You had to do it expertly. The way I felt, I could even miss hell.

I got myself home and phoned Dr O'Connor who was like a gymnast at keeping people away from death. He asked me athletic questions to keep my attention, to bring out my grievance against life. He brought it out like a sting. I kept all this to myself and put on dark glasses to hide my distress from the others if I could. But my son had enough pain of his own and

wanted to go back to the hospital. He couldn't make it, not even for half a day. The ambulance was called. They took him away. And I realised anger had made me want to destroy myself – anger that he'd ruined himself and caused me so much anguish. And I could never show him that anger, because he was sick.

18. Occupational Hazards

by

Connie

When I was fourteen, one of my most trusted friends was a black kid called Garry. He was handsome, with a remarkably small nose, and he looked good in his Grandad's caps. We would smoke hash and drink lager, and fall asleep on his bed where he lived on a Peckham estate. I was completely safe and he treated me like one of the boys. He got on to hard drugs and I got into deception, namely pickpocketing. One day I bumped into him in Camberwell and he was babbling. He had lost his mind. That was my first heartbreak at the power and grip drugs had on everyday life.

Tony Terner was good-looking, kind, with a lisp that gave him a kind of charm. His mother and father had brought him up well and helped in the community to give delinquent kids a chance of holidays, like camping and such. He had so much potential but, years later, I spotted him at a South London N.A. meeting. He looked like a skeleton and his eyes were brilliant blue and protruding out of his head. He spoke of starting afresh and rehab and stuff, but I don't think he made it.

One day, halfway through my sentence, Modal was due to be released. She had completed her sentence and walked down the corridor of Holloway to the dining-hall to see us girls for the last time. She gave breakfast a miss and gave her mates a hug. I saw for the first time why she was called Modal. Her six months incarceration, off drugs with rest and regular meals, had given her some of her natural beauty back. And a beauty she was. She walked her cat walk in her skirt, suit and riding boots. She lifted her skirt up as she went and revealed red suspenders and stockings. She loved doing that behind the big, blonde officers' backs. It was so funny, especially when they caught on. A few hours later, she was found dead on a fix of a minute amount of heroin. Her tolerance had disintegrated. The officers and all the people who knew her loved her spirit. She was so alive.

Another friend of mine was also a strong presence. She was a natural leader, but like many, missed the starting gun and wound up on drugs, crime and in prison. We would wile away the hours, locked in our cell, me on the top bunk, her on the bottom, writing songs and singing out of the window. The women didn't mind. Maybe it helped them to forget their worries for a while. Then when it was peaceful, the wind-up merchants would start. One would shout, 'Up the IRA' in an Irish accent, and another would say, 'Fuck the IRA' in an Irish accent.

A beautiful young girlfriend of mine went on holiday and her boyfriend was left alone with the German shepherd dog. He o/d'ed and died and the dog was left locked in the house with him for four weeks. The poor dog had to eat the body. When police finally broke in, there were maggots all over and the poor dog had to be shot on the spot. Maybe the fact I was briefed on the horrors of fixing was what saved me from the fate of the devil doing his worst job on me as well. My friend Melanie told me she had been in a drug house where the bath was filled with brown water. A woman o/d'ed and died leaning over the bathroom sink. She was systematically raped while dead, and when the police found her, she had so many different sperms in her, it was impossible to tell how many people had fucked her.

One of my worst horrors is the thought of having to queue at the DSS. The last time I went, a guy was telling his friends he might have an amputation due to fixing his leg. His friends, to my horror, were encouraging him to do so; telling him he would get the perks of a cripple. When I went to the post office, they came in with the guy and carried him over to a chair in the corner of the room and went over to cash his money for him. When they got it, they ran out and left him on the chair. He couldn't walk, so he couldn't go after them. He just cried helplessly like a baby. By then I was beyond the point of being shocked easily.

When I stuck close to my boyfriend, he took care of finances and frequently came across parcels of jewellery amongst other things. We went to crack houses to sell gold.

I met a drug dealer who wrote to me while I was in prison. When I got out, we met up and he handed me kilos of heroin as a gift. I gave it back and explained that I wasn't into it that bad. It turned out, he wanted me as his steady girl. He was too kinky for my liking. He'd done drugs while doing a head stand and tried to get me into orgies as well as sex parties and prostitution. I knew he had to go. My life off the rails took me from one shady situation to another. He poured petrol through my letterbox and threatened to kill me. I heard recently that he is a born-again Christian.

When I was seventeen, I never knew much about intravenous use of drugs. I didn't really need a graphic account of how it goes, but whilst being on the medical unit of Holloway for court reports, I was placed in a dorm with a murderer, an alcoholic, a heroin addict and a cancer patient. I had five safety pins, and on my return from exercise one day, I noticed the addict engrossed in something on her top bunk. She looked like she was really enjoying what she was doing, and when I got closer, she was pushing needles and pins into her veins. She said it was something most heroin addicts loved doing if they couldn't get the real thing. When she didn't have needles or pins, she went frantic to find one. That memory has stuck with me for over twenty years.

My brother used to hit me for money to do drugs with this London-born Jamaican guy. He was feared in a part of South London. He was a psycho and the crack enhanced his madness. He would smoke his drugs and then accuse people in the room of stealing them. No one would be allowed to leave and he would have a knife in one hand and a hammer in the other. He would get the horrors and sweat, claiming he could hear voices outside. He would often hurt one or all the people in the room. He terrorised them and made them steal, borrow and beg money to pay him. Once, someone attacked him back and he was axed in the head. He lived, but was a new person after that.

*

I thank God that He has saved me from that life. Asking God for his help and guidance with a simple prayer turned my life around. God heard all my prayers and took pity on me. He protects me from the evils of the world. He gives me what I need and he guides me when I am in temptation. God is love.

19. Eastwood

by

Michael Hoff

It was 2.30 a.m. and I was sitting in my tiny Manhattan apartment staring at a blank page on my computer screen. As a writer I was turning into a total flop. My eyes drifted to the vodka bottle on my desk – at least I was still good at one thing. I took a hefty swig, burped loudly and typed 'Can no one stop the mad procession?' across the top of the screen. If I dropped dead that night (and I certainly felt that I might), it struck me that this would be seen as a kind of bizarre mayday beacon – a final, enigmatic distress call.

Music seeped from the radio. Deep Purple were singing something about the thrill of the chase. I couldn't really identify with the lyrics. I assumed they were about men and women pursuing each other with sex and romance on their minds. Such things were beyond my capabilities, I was too busy riding reefers into the future and fleeing from the creatures that appeared whenever the vodka supply ran low. I got up, turned the radio off and sat down again. To my dismay the screen was now filled with machine code. I pecked away at the keyboard in an attempt to clear it, failed, rebooted the computer, and was greeted with the words: 'I am on my way. I love you so much.'

What the hell was this? What kind of computer virus told you that it loved you? Cursing out loud, I tried rebooting the computer, only to get the same message again.

'Bugger everything,' I said. I was gearing up for a serious self-pity session when a bloodcurdling wail suddenly erupted from the alley that ran alongside the western wall of my building. It sounded horribly like a child being strangled. I got up, prized open the window and stared into the garbage-strewn alley five stories below. A desperate, forlorn wail rose up out of the darkness. I peered downwards, but saw only blackness. Again the cry came from far below. Oh God, I couldn't endure this all night! It was just too sad; I could identify only too well with the cry of the forsaken. Some poor creature was down there amongst the junk and debris, frightened, hungry and alone. I slammed the window shut and was rescrewing the bolt when the awful cry broke out from behind me, shattering the silence with the intensity of a police siren.

I froze for an instant and then reached compulsively for the Smirnoff bottle, sucking greedily at its neck like a hungry baby. My ears had surely deceived me, for the sound seemed to have come from right outside my apartment door – but only a moment ago it had been down in the alley!

I lurched towards the door, shot the dead bolt and opened it. The cry burst forth once more, but now it came from behind me – from inside the flat! I whirled around and saw a small, grey cat sitting on the floor no more than three feet from where I stood.

Part stoned, part drunk and wholly astonished, I slammed the door and stood in the hallway peering stupidly at my own front door. Yes, I was pretty high, but not that high, surely? Could this be new, improved alcoholic hallucinations?

I fished a cigarette out of my pocket, lit it, and began blowing plumes of smoke into the gloomy hallway. I'd shut the window almost immediately after I'd heard the cat's last cry from the alley, and then that wail had erupted from behind me. I estimated the elapsed time at a very liberal twenty seconds – twenty seconds to get from the alley, sixty feet below, straight into my apartment. I walked to the top of the stairs and peered down the stairwell. I knew there was no access from that alley to the entrance of my apartment block on East 7th Street, and thus the cat could not have come through the entrance doors. But there were no other entrances to the building – except perhaps in the basement.

Fearing the onset of madness, I felt that I had to find out how this cat had got in. A small hole, somewhere far below, would at least explain how the creature had entered the building. I tottered off down the stairs and eventually found myself below street level, standing in the pitch dark and fumbling for a light switch. Befuddled by booze and befogged by pot, I suddenly forgot what I was doing or where I was. All I knew was that it was dark. Where the hell was I? Throwing all decorum to the winds I let out a strangled cry. 'Help!'

A door opened ahead of me and light flooded the hallway as a heavily-bearded man shuffled out in his carpet slippers. I had never seen so much hair on someone's face before. Only the area around his eyes and nose could be seen; the rest was a riot of spiky, greying hair, bursting from his face and falling halfway down his chest. To my dismay I noticed tendrils of smoke curling out of it in all directions. I backed away a step.

'Whadaya want?' said the man. His beard quivered and a cloud of smoke billowed from it.

I cleared by throat and pointed. 'Um, your beard's on fire,' I said.

The man glared at me and spat. A tiny stub of smouldering paper and tobacco flew from his mouth.

'You haven't seen a cat down here, have you?' I stammered, uncertainly.

'A cat? Are you the guy from number 15?' he asked.

'That's right,' I said, smiling bravely.

'Jesus wept,' he said, turning around and slamming the door behind him. I had just enough time to see where the hallway light switch was before the door closed. I turned it on and gazed about, but there were no holes in the walls or floorboards, and the bearded one didn't strike me as a cat lover.

Ridiculous explanations jostled for attention in my mind as I trudged back up the stairs. Perhaps the cat had come in through a window, been shooed out of a ground floor apartment and had made its way up to mine instead, all in twenty seconds. The cat had found a hole in the base of the building and had done it that way. The cat was one hell of a high jumper. The cat had a set of keys?

It was hopeless. Twenty seconds – to do what? Fly through the walls on a broomstick? This was getting ridiculous. Filled with a sudden resolve, I opened my apartment door and stared about the interior. There was nothing there. Time for the hospital – tomorrow. I closed the door, shot the deadbolt, and sat down in an armchair.

And that was when I got my first good look at Eastwood.

Prowling around under my loft bed was a very thin grey cat. The shade of its colouring was difficult to determine because it was coated with dust and filth, but far more disturbing was just how thin it was. I could see every bone in its body. The creature's haunches stood out like pyramids through the filthy fur, and the entire rib cage could be clearly seen. I swallowed hard. The animal approached me, cautiously, and brushed past my leg. I could feel the bones even through my jeans. I put my hand out and touched fur; greasy, gritty and matted, but fur nonetheless. This was no hallucination; this was an animal starving to death. I leapt into action with the speed and resourcefulness available only to the demented. Pausing only to grab my keys I was out of the door and on my way to the all-night delicatessen at the end of the block.

I arrived at the store at a sort of lopsided gallop and stared wildly around me. The night manager, Aziz, gave me a friendly smile. I was a regular nocturnal visitor and there was no doubt in my mind that he knew I was an alcoholic. After all, normal people do not visit stores in the dead of night shaking like a Gerry Anderson puppet with Parkinson's disease and then totter off with bag-loads of beer. But Aziz's smile rapidly switched to a worried frown when I approached the counter with two large tins of cat food.

'One dollar seventy five, please,' he croaked, uncertainly.

I cantered off into the night, leaving Aziz with a look of serious concern on his face. No doubt he thought that in a state of alcoholic dementia I had got cat food and beer cans mixed up. As I arrived back at my block it occurred to me that even now he might be calling Bellevue hospital to report that a lunatic had just left his store with the intention of trying to drink a tin of Purina Cat Chow.

The cat looked somewhat surprised when I arrived back soaked in sweat and panting like a rabid dog, but it soon forgot about that as I began spooning food into a soup bowl. I placed the bowl on the floor, set a bowl of water down beside it and then collapsed back into my chair and began sucking on the vodka bottle again.

The cat had its back to me, but the speed with which its head was jerking up and down indicated that it was wolfing down the food at a rate of knots. This rear view also confirmed that I had a bona fide tomcat on my hands, complete with all his credentials. He finished his meal in double quick time, gave himself a cursory wash and brush up, and then walked across to where I sat. On an impulse I christened him Eastwood. He was straight out of a Sergio Leone Western – right from the scar on his face to the lean gunslinger hips, the slinky walk and the ultra-cool demeanour with which he conducted himself despite his somewhat desperate situation.

I checked the vodka bottle – it was empty. Incredibly, in my haste to feed the cat I'd forgotten to buy any beer for myself. But all this sudden activity had exhausted me. I climbed wearily up the step ladder to my loft bed and flopped on to the mattress. A moment later Eastwood appeared, and arranged himself languidly at my feet. I gazed at him fondly for a moment, and then in the grand tradition of drunks the world over, I passed out.

I awoke the next morning, half doubting what had happened, but there was Eastwood nonetheless, regarding me impassively from the end of the bed. It was 8.30 a.m., definitely time to get the hell out of the place, get my new friend a litter box, and myself a drink.

The morning, however, did not go well for me. I found to my horror that my bank balance had shrunk to just $40. By the time I had bought Eastwood a litter box, litter, and enough food to last him a week this had been reduced to $12. That was enough for just a pint of vodka. My heart sank. In the last few weeks I'd have finished that off before lunchtime.

I returned to the apartment and Eastwood did his slalom act around my legs again as I spooned out the Purina, which he attacked with the same manic determination that he had shown the previous night. I felt a definite affinity with this cat. We were both desperados, he on the run from hunger and neglect, me from reality and the onset of delirium tremens. I poured myself a hearty slug from the vodka bottle and set about rolling the first joint of the day.

Even by six o'clock that evening Eastwood looked a lot better. Indeed, he seemed to have gained four pounds and somehow acquired a new coat, for his fur had miraculously become thick and glossy. I on the other hand, only had to hold out my madly shaking hands in front of me to deduce that I was getting worse by the minute. I eventually slipped into a fitful half-sleep and awoke at around nine o'clock to find Eastwood perched on my desk and staring intently at the computer screen. He gave me a brief 'miaow' as I approached and then hopped off the chair and padded away across the room.

I sat down in front of the computer somewhat confused. I couldn't remember turning it on. Once again I found myself staring at a screenful of machine code. I scrolled down through the gobbledegook, and was suddenly confronted with a new message: Where me?

Out of the corner of my eye, I noticed Eastwood at the far end of the room, sitting bolt upright and perfectly still, staring directly at me. My guts told me something very odd was going on, but my head told me a drink would fix that, so I went to the refrigerator. To my horror there was only a half inch of vodka left in the bottle. In a panic I downed the precious liquid in one, but it was not enough to stop a set of icy fingers gripping my stomach. I broke out in a cold sweat. Now just time stood between me and the terror of the DTs, which I could already feel creeping up on me like a gang of malicious schoolchildren playing grandmother's footsteps.

Muddle-headed and desperate, I found myself staring at the computer again. 'Where me?' said the plaintive message. Deprived of my precious vodka, I became entirely unsympathetic.

'You on a hard disk, mate,' I typed with savage sarcasm.

I rolled a joint, hoping that the marijuana would make me drowsy enough to cancel out the jitters that were closing in on me. I lit up and inhaled greedily, only to feel a sharp pain in my right side, just below the rib cage. I knew immediately that it was my liver, even though I had never experienced such intense pain there before. I had heard horrible stories of alcoholics dying in hospital from burst livers, blood oozing from their eyes, ears and nostrils. I began compulsively rubbing my palms together and muttering 'Oh no' to myself in an urgent whisper. I put my head in my hands and tried to will the pain to go away, will the swollen organ to settle down. I could feel my pulse racing. I was convinced that my heart was about to burst out of my chest like some bloody fist. Suddenly, I felt very sick. I lurched to my feet, gasping in pain, and heaved an evil black liquid into the sink. I slumped against the wall, my eyes closed and my head lolling, while the rusty, metallic taste of blood lingered in my mouth. I sank to the floor, my legs too wobbly to support me any longer. How much blood had I thrown up? Whether from shock, loss of blood, exhaustion, cannabis, alcohol or a combination of all of them, I felt suddenly incredibly tired. My eyelids refused to respond to my urgent messages to stay open. I had to get to the phone and call an ambulance, but I knew I wasn't going to. Instead, I was going to sleep, per chance to die, and there was nothing I could do about it.

When I came round I was lying on my back on the floor. But there was no feeling of returning from unconsciousness, no disorientation. There was just Eastwood. He was lying on my chest, purring like a power station and staring sphinxlike into the darkness beyond my windows.

I no longer felt any panic. There were no jitters, nor was there any shakiness or sweating, just a feeling of complete calm. I climbed the steps, lay down on the bed, and fell immediately into a deep and dreamless sleep.

*

I woke up to a bright, chilly morning and lay staring out the far window at the houses on East 8th Street. The idea of a drink didn't even enter my mind.

I really hoped that Eastwood was still with me – but of course, he wasn't. I had simply passed two whole days in a state of alcoholic hallucination. The cat, the computer – none of it had happened. 'God looks after fools and drunks' they say. I wanted to believe that. I wanted to believe that someone or something actually cared. I spent forty-five minutes searching the place in a ridiculous attempt to find a hole in the wall or the floorboards to explain how Eastwood might have left. I even checked the windows, although I already knew they were securely bolted against the icy New York winter. Eventually, I gave up. Eastwood had been a hallucination.

Later that day, I went into hospital with chronic gastritis and a critically swollen liver. A doctor told me how lucky I was – one more bottle of vodka might well have killed me. The mad procession had been stopped, just in time.

When I got home I sat down and stared forlornly at the bag of cat litter I had bought, and the box I had put it in, at the three unopened tins of cat food by the sink – total cost $28, or three pints of vodka and a one-way trip on the oblivion express. But as I sat there, an acrid smell drifted to my nostrils. Confused, I reached out and moved the grit about in the litter box – it was damp, and buried deep inside were the little clumps of stool that my friend had left behind.

I stared long and hard as the tears came, slowly at first, and then in a flood.

'Thank you, God,' I said.

20. Story

by

Deborah Bosley

My mother never bothered. I know, I know, it's not her fault. Well, not all of it. Any arsehole could tell you it's not what happens, it's how you react to it. I reacted to her and everything since in the only way I knew how. I got out of it. I remember getting out of it in this room twenty years ago, me and Maggie skinning up and smoking out of the window so that Mum couldn't smell it. Of course she could smell it, but what was she going to say? She's been scared of me since I was about twelve. God, we used to piss ourselves, me and Maggie. Those were the days when the gear still worked, when getting stoned meant laughing till it hurt. It used to make everything so funny, now it just makes me so anxious that my heart bangs in my chest. I wonder why it stopped working? I wish I could go back to that time, there must have been a moment when turning back would have been an option, when it would have made the difference. Knowing me, I'd have ignored it.

It's the same with booze, that just turned on me too. You give it the best years of your life and, slowly, it turns on you like a bad dog. Somewhere between promiscuous sex and blackouts I turned into a sad, wrung-out depressive who can't handle her own feelings and self-medicates to make them go away. I'm not fussy about what I use to chase them away, anything will do. Booze and spliff were my favourites, then I discovered coke. It was the biggest kick. I could get from nought to sixty in twelve seconds. Talk? You couldn't shut me up. I was pleased to see everybody, asking after them, their loved ones. Fresh out of charm school, you should have seen me. Fast forward a year and I don't want to waste time talking to no bugger unless they have a wrap stashed about their person, and I'm pretty blunt at getting them to come across. I'll nod impatiently while they make polite conversation, but about a minute and a half is my max until I just come out with it and say: 'Got any gear?'

There's got to be some law of opposites going on here. Some strange magnetic, repelling force. You know, the way a thing is in the beginning, will, if you keep at it for long enough, end up being the opposite and, God knows, I'm tenacious when it comes to a drug. The great circle of life, eh? Round and round in circles, never going anywhere. No, tell a lie, you do go somewhere. If you really try hard, you'll get to rock bottom. Trust me.

It's not like you can just go back and start again, because each time you're further from where you want to be. And each time you've got less fight left in you to get up and have another crack.

Regrets are pointless, but I tell you what I'd love to know. I love to know what I'd look like if I hadn't been on the lash for twenty years. It's a miracle I don't look older than I do. Mum's got good skin, so I must get it from her. But when I think of the millions of fags and drinks and spliffs and lines that have been walloped into this face since I was a teenager it makes you think. When people talk about addiction they go on about the corrosion of the spirit and how we suffer emotionally. I sit there thinking, yeah, yeah, yeah, why doesn't somebody just come out and say, oh and by the way, your looks get shot to shit. I tell you friends, you do not get a face this dried out and raddled without serious effort. It's like anything in life, you've got to put the work in. You can really see it the morning after a bender. You look in the mirror and it's as if you've been wrung out like a sponge, every last bit of juice and goodness just squeezed out of you. You think this looks bad, you should have seen me when I got here on Tuesday. Jesus fucking Christ, talk about a ropey old bird. I might just as well have had bender-binger tattooed on my head. Rough ain't the word, I tell you.

So do you want to know how I got here, then? How I managed to fuck it up so completely and utterly that I end up back in my old room at my Mum's at thirty-seven years of age, potless, homeless, loveless, jobless and brainless? It started, like I said, a long time ago, but it ended on Monday. I've sworn a thousand times that I'd never do it again, but I don't think I felt total defeat until Tuesday morning. Anyway, it was a pretty average Monday morning, up at eight o'clock and having a spliff while I put my make-up on and got ready for the job which I'd still miraculously hung onto. I work in a restaurant in the West End, a huge bloody place like an aeroplane hangar with enough room to do something like 250 covers on a busy lunch. I'm the meeter and greeter, the girl that checks your booking, shows you to your table and tells you to enjoy your meal. It's a bloody mercy that I don't have to carry plates as I'm so off my face. Drunkenness and mind alteration had their uses in my job, though. Once toasted, I could make out I really was pleased to see all those mobile phone wielding people with very important jobs and good clothes, who can afford to pay through the nose for a second-rate lunch.

Everyone at work knew I was a total maniac for getting off it but, in one way or another, most of us were at it. It's one of the great illusions that keep you going; you see other people doing it, sometimes more than you, and it makes you think I'm okay, I'm not as bad as them. Allow for the fact that most serious boozers and junkies restrict themselves to the socially like-minded. The hard core hang together. There are of course those immaculate souls who know when to stop. But your proper drunk, your paid-up addict never reaches the finishing line. It's like being in a race with no end. You get those moments of lucidity and you think, I really do need to pack this in, it's never going to get any better, but then you have another drink and keep fostering the illusion that you will grapple with the greed until you've shown it who's boss. Well, Monday finally showed me who was boss.

Like I said, I'm stoned before I get to work at ten, check the bookings, make sure all the menus have got the specials on them, check the tables. A typical Monday morning, we're all telling our war stories from the weekend, how out of it we were, whom we slept with, who got chucked, who fell in love. It's a great trade for that, catering, you can hide a multitude of sins with a lot of jokes and stories. Roy, the floor manager, was in a good mood, because his old boyfriend whom he's been trying to evict for months, finally moved out the day before, so he ceremoniously invites a select group of the floor staff to have a glass of champagne before the first bookings show up. If I hadn't had that first drink, I'd probably have been all right, well, able to wait till the shift finished at half past three till I had a drink, but it tasted so good that I went and had another. I've got a bit of an understanding with one of our barmen, Victor. He's Italian and very shy, and when he first started work, I kind of looked out for him, so he's always been good about coming across with the liquor. Lots of customers, especially at lunchtime order just a glass of champagne, so there's always an open bottle somewhere, and on Monday I had this thirst that just wouldn't quit. After four, Victor tells me maybe to take it easy, but I reassure him that I'm fine, that I'm really enjoying myself. Enjoying myself, my arse! I'm on a big old slope and I know it, but I've started and I just can't stop. I've always been a fairly diligent piss-head, you know, doing the job well between drinks, but this Monday we're busy and the more bolloxed I get the more I'm slipping on the job, and then I'm so fucked I couldn't give a shit and I've got people queuing up waiting to be shown to tables, and a sea of arms waving credit cards at me wanting to pay, but I'm on a mission and I just keep doing this straight line from the bar to the loo, the loo to the bar. The loo, of course, because I've just bought a G from slippery Tony, who lunches with us every day. He's our resident dealer, and trade from the waiting staff alone keeps him in Gucci suits. After one particularly big line I decide to make a heroic effort and pull it together and clear the backlog of cards and people queuing. I was whittling through them double quick and would have been fine had not that silly cow with the stupid hair extension who works at the film editing suite in Wardour Street not made that bitchy comment. She's waved her card at me a few times and I've blanked her, then when I get to her table she says something like, 'If you're not too busy powdering your nose, I'd like to pay my bill, please.' Cheeky cow. Admittedly, I was sniffing like a bastard and there's stuff falling out of my nose, but where, I'd like to know were her manners. Normally I'd have managed a tight-lipped smile before turning and cursing under my breath, but fuelled by champagne and cocaine, a near maniacal defiance overcame me and I found myself telling her in a sing-song voice to go blow it out of her arse. In all my scrapes with customers over the years, and there have been a few, I have never been so carelessly and happily rude. I don't know what made me do it. Maybe it was that long glossy hair extension, or the perfect, 'I don't smoke, do drugs or drink' complexion, but something about this woman really gave me the pip. As if that wasn't horror enough, I've got bad timing working against me. A voice behind me says, 'Let me take care of that,' and Roy's perfectly manicured hand reaches onto the table and takes the waiting credit card. He shoots me that look, you know, get your arse over here so I can bollock you, so I meekly trail behind him to the cashier's desk. He's so angry he can't speak, but his look says it all. I want to mumble an apology, because Roy has been good to me and pissing him off is the last thing I want to do, but I'm so mute with charlie I can't get a word out. As the credit card machine prints out the chit to be signed, he turns and says to me, 'Get your stuff and go home.'

21. The Prisoner

by

Esta Laya

I told you I loved you. I told you on a cold Monday morning when the sky hung low over London. You said it then. 'I do not love you, I do not want you.' But I didn't hear you.

Despite your defiance of me I fabricated a loving you, and that loving you has taken possession of me. I have allowed the fiction of what I alone have created to rob me of my hours, of my days, of my nights. I dream of you. I spend my hours living in your universe; but you are not here, you are gone from me. Still I crave you and that craving eats away my life. The days, the weeks, pass. Longing fills me up and my self is left undone. My work is abandoned, my bills are unpaid, my life a byway. I hide in your being. I ache for you. But you are nothing. I am buried in a tomb of my own making. I am its prisoner.

We'd played games for months, you and I – the 'this and that' of flirtation, the promise of what might be.

It started with a kiss on lips; lips that didn't want to be kissed; lips that remembered the violence of unwanted loving. What did you know of that? All there was for you was a woman, the night light defacing the lines of age. Oh God, that kiss; I am held tight by the bounds of that kiss, by the strength of your arms; arms that deny me now, a mouth that stays away from mine, a body that tightens should I come too close. And yet you have given me love, you have given back the gift of passion. And when jealousy stares at me with its watery yellow green eye, I see you with other women; women who touch you in places I would like to go, women you touch in places where I long to be touched.

I see the curve of your back, and my hands ache to linger on you. But you don't want me. I am denied you, but I am tied and shackled to you by my own manacles of desire.

How did it begin, this loving?

The truth of it? We danced the dance you and I, that very first time we met. A *coup de foudre*, we both felt it; I know that, the shock of desire.

Perhaps, if I am honest, it was unwelcome. After the long years of a relentless penetration of my unwilling body I wanted only emptiness. It has a name, the kind of sex, it is called marriage. What did you know of that, on a cold afternoon in London when you seduced me with tales of hot Andalusian summers; your years in Spain? Your eyes shone with promise, and I could have died in your voice. You painted a canvas of ochre earth slashed by deep gorges, of crimson flowers, and singing yellow, of wild white roses. Men that smelt of sweat and sex, of women who twitched a slender hip in flounced skirts, proud breasts and flared nostrils, priests and piety, forgotten pagan ritual cleaned up as worship. Blood and lust wrapped in the inky chocolate of flamenco, the howl of the human voice, the snap of the castanet. I ate it up, all of it.

You are a photographer, you brought me just a few of your photographs. A man of grey, grey eyes, grey hair; you wore a black coat that day. I saw your hands and knuckles that were red raw. I wondered at that, at the knuckles. They didn't lay flat as a gentleman's hands should, a gentleman's hands should lie flat. Those knuckles protruded like unkempt sods. I thought he punches walls, that man. He punches walls when he is hurt.

We talked. Your photographs lay next to me. I realised as I looked at those faces, at those bodies, that each time you snapped your shutter, you stole a little part of each one of them – making them the less – for what you had taken you had made your own; a smile, a tear, a breast, an arm, a leg, a hip. Old and young, like a thief you robbed them.

It was easy, it was nice, tea turned to wine, and a quiet afternoon seeped into night. London was silver under a quiet moon when we left the café. I drove you home through rich London with its white houses belted tight against the night.

It was then, in your white, clean London, you kissed me. I expected a shake of a hand. Instead I got your mouth. I tasted it, and like a drug, I still long for the feel of it again.

You left me shaken. You stood with your head on one side, watching me as I sat stunned in my car.

We played games on the e-mail, talking about love. You told me that we have the suspicion, even when we are in love, that it must be too good to be real, because it is so good, and because we wonder how we can deserve it. And of course we don't deserve it, and that by understanding that love is impossible we are unable to forget that we are going to die. I said that you were wrong. We have the right to trust in love. I told you it was worth the risk.

We played for three wonderful months. You held out the promise of sex. You roamed over me; eyes, lips, hands that touched enough to entice.

And then no more. It was over for you.

It happened on one Friday afternoon. You pulled me to you and you held me, almost there, almost. I could feel my breasts against your chest, your mouth playing its beautiful games. But then you whispered 'Go', and I knew. You had decided.

You are no liar, you said it, the words I dread: 'I will never give you what you want.'

I left you then. I will never forget your face that day as you stood watching me as I walked away from you.

Last night I awoke and you were inside me. You were moving in me but you were not there; there was nothing, just the phantom of my yearning.

I am, of course, the older woman. You are still in your prime, young enough to lure a girl, old enough to know what to do with her. Even as I write the words I feel the wound of my rivalry. I see you deep within that soft place that is woman; where she bears her child, where she feels her sex. I know your face, I know how you would look, I know how you would love the scent of it all, but it can never be my desire that will welcome you. But can I stop? Will I stop? Such is my denial, such is my addiction. For this barren singular loving doesn't choose its companion wisely. It may ask for the silk of giving, but it can only reward us, the unloved, with its cruelty.

You would say stop. For God's sake stop. I do not want you. We are on parallel lines. That is all there is. I speak of you as my friend, but we can't be friends for whilst I want you how can you give me friendship?

In the time I knew you, you gave me back my life. I knew joy because of you. I knew the hiss of happiness, the dry mouth of anticipation, the tension that we hide in a barb. I played with others like I had never played before – even when I loved sex, even before I saw the act of love as a weapon to bruise and tear my flesh.

Still I hold on to my desire for you. I regret none of it. I exist in my fantasy world, a world you inhabit, and I count the days till I will see you.

You are a mujahadin; at least I shall make you so for the purposes of our tale. You carry your camera like a gun, aiming at the young, the old and even children, promising them the happy ever after. Your happy ever after is the grainy print of a photograph. You do not do it for the cause, for Ireland, for Palestine, for the Arab, for the American. You do it for you.

You came into that café, hidden in that big coat. You came to me with the coil of the damaged within you. And I, like the jack-in-the-box, jumped out to greet you.

You assume identity. No one knows your real name, you travel on a different passport. To each of us, each person in each life, you give a piece of you, a little package that they think is you, that they think is their own. For you are generous of spirit. But you can never reveal yourself. You live behind a veil, as if the sight of the whole of you will consume you. You carry your sadness with you like a cloak, and I cannot pull it off you. I try and you draw it tighter, turning me away from you.

Would that I could let you go. I cannot – or perhaps will not. Love has no teacher. It drives itself, and takes no passengers. So, I too, I travel alone with my heart and with my soul undone.

22. Tell Me

by

Steven Kupfer

When the day becomes a little tawdry, about half past three or so, I like to take my walk. The street outside the house I rent is almost empty but I can count on a couple of neighbours lying down in the shadow of their hedges, and a stranger or two whimpering for water on the roadway. I nod as I pass, indifferent to their modes of response.

When I reach the great trees that tower over our community I turn and look back; always there are one or two hopeful travellers who are following me at a careful distance ten yards or so behind. They stop when I do and as I search their faces their eyes avoid mine. It is as it should be. I examine them carefully and they allow themselves to be searched by my gaze. They are hopeful but do not dare betray their hope and almost always it is misplaced.

Sometimes my interest mounts and I beckon, the merest whisper of a gesture, a finger crooked, my arm barely extended, and one of them comes shuffling and huddling, quick and obsequious. I signal him or her to stop a yard or two away and I sniff, showing what I expect of them, while I explore the air. My thought is not whether they smell, but how much and of what. I can read a shameful history into those smells. If their odour is tolerable and does not hint at too much horror and ignominy, I signal again; an invitation, and their eyes, which have begun to shine with hope, sometimes overflow and let a tear trickle through the grime.

I continue my walk in the shade of the great trees, more slowly now that I am under their towering peace, and a companion shuffles beside me, on my left, a little more than an arm's length away.

Always they wait for my words and I choose my moment, the time to speak and invoke an answer. 'Tell me your story,' I say, and my words are meant to unlock the tiny treasure of life and time my companion bears within. If I have chosen well and hit upon the proper moment, I will get it all, everything they carry with them and they are glad to give it up, surrender everything even though they have no assurance of return. They have heard the jingle in my pockets and it helps them to words they did not know were available, to turns of phrase that cast their lives in forms they do not recognise.

It is not always so. 'Enough!' I say then, throwing out the word like a whip crack, and the halting discourse stops, its speaker cringes. I dig my hand in my pocket, pull out a coin or two and throw them down in the roadway and walk on, my pace quickened by my anger. But often all is as I have wished it to be, and a story of misfortune unfolds.

These tales are always sad, calendars of misery, a lifetime's worth in half an hour. I need never enquire about the end for always I know it already. The end is always here on this afternoon road that winds under these tall trees – a walk beside a man of medium height, fair-haired but balding, black-suited, whose air is one of stern justice – for so I see myself.

23. Bad Girl

by

Patrice Chaplin

She would have left the crypt of the central London church without anyone knowing otherwise if her exorbitantly styled shoe with its skyscraper heel hadn't got trapped in the run of the iron steps. That's how Terry caught her.

'Too tough?' He freed the shoe. It was a beautiful, elegant object, art deco design, pink and gold. One of its kind. Like her. She was certainly beautiful but it was still daylight. It took the night to put on her lights.

She gave Terry the kind of answer she thought he wanted to hear and would have carried on up the stairs to the street. He'd expected her to come back into the meeting. He gave her the shoe.

'This isn't about Cinderella, sweetheart. There's no fairy godmother for what you've got.'

And in spite of her hurry she hesitated. He obviously cared for her. 'I need to –'

'Everything you need is here,' he said.

Below them in the crowded room the AA meeting was coming to an end.

'The first drink is the drink you don't take, Charlotte.'

She slipped the shoe on. 'One day at a time.' Then she clattered up and onto the street rushing to the place where she needed to be.

Terry could still feel the softness of the shoe. It left an imprint in his hand that was slow to fade. That shoe. Not like any other he'd seen. It was the only thing he knew about her. She wore amazing shoes.

She ran through the homegoing crowds at Victoria Station and jumped between the closing doors of the short, dirty South London train. 'Does this go to Balham?'

She could see her reflection in the window as the train crossed the

Thames. Lovely face, tomboy look. But she needed the night to bring out her vibrancy. Like some glossy jungle creature she thrived on the night. Her daylight life was an unimportant mystery. The homecoming men were surprised at the way she could run on those shoes. Some women did fit effortlessly into the highest heel until it became an extension of their leg, their life. She was one of those.

The singing teacher was known for his star clients and his central London lessons were always booked. He had to fit her in at the end of his day at his home. He still lived on the edge of the railway track and as she did the scales the trains rushed by high across the window. She loved that room, its polished wooden floors, mineral water bottles and rows of glasses, spindly sofas, huge mirrors, turn of the century posters and its hope.

He was pleased with the increased energy in the top section of her voice. And her rhythm. But then she was born with that. But will she make it? Had she passed the West End audition he'd squeezed her into? He tried to say singing can be a dream for most people. He said it more fervently when he saw her writing the cheque. She tried to hide the fact it was a struggle to pay for the lessons. She wanted to be a blues singer. The singing lesson was the most important thing in her life. There would be no life however if she slipped alcoholically and took that first drink.

'You don't think I'm going to make it, do you?'

He looked away and talked about something called luck. In his world it was a very real commodity. He embraced her at the door. She disturbed him. He wasn't sure she even had a place to live.

Ten o'clock, Victoria Station and the longed for darkness had come. Drinking cappuccino at the platform buffet, she watched the night passengers taking their trains and the queue moving onto the boat train for France. Finally, she saw Phil, her friend, carrying a flute and a narrow travel bag.

'Come with me, Charlotte. A bit of street performing on the left bank and then down to the Midi.'

He reminded her they did all right last time.

She hesitated. The impulse – just going always appealed to her. Then she considered the singing lessons. Phil gave her his key and asked her to feed his cat.

The luxury train pulled in beside the boat train, took their attention. It had about it a style and romance copied from another time. Passengers were already seated in the dining-car with its shaded pink table lights and advertisements. Waiters served bottles of wine and sparkling water. Glamorous passengers with real luggage were escorted to their compartments. Charlotte felt as though she'd slipped back into the thirties. The other side of the platform however was very much of this time, and teenagers loaded with rucksacks jostled to get last minute sandwiches and cans of coke. She kissed Phil goodbye and offered him the last of her money.

'Keep it for those coffees. You're doing great,' he said, gently. 'And if you're stuck use my flat.'

She would have left the station but was drawn back to the luxury train. She asked where it was going. France, into Switzerland, the Simplon Pass, Milan, then across to Venice. She jumped on, sat in the dining-car and enjoyed a joyous high moment of adventure. A waiter placed a glass of champagne in front of her. She did not dare look at it. In the reflection of the window she could see the caring face of Terry, her AA friend. She said, quietly, 'I call to remembrance my song and in the night I commune with mine own heart and search out my spirits.'

The champagne glass correctly frosted and full of the sparkling light gold liquid she loved, that she'd kill for. Just this one glass. Who'd know?

She could hear Eddie before she saw him. Cool attitude, persuasive voice, Manhattan. The voice had started less up-market. She guessed Brooklyn. He was half arguing in a habitual intimate way with a woman, his wife. Charlotte could see her. Dressy, exuding wealth and status. It was a big quarrel about something small.

'But, Eddie, get the goddam paper. Why don't they carry it on here? These trains aren't a patch on the old.' Then she turned her anger on the bread roll on her plate. 'What are you supposed to do with it?'

'How about eat it, honey?'

'This hard?'

'What do you want me to do? Sue them?'

'Just get me the *Herald Tribune*.' Her tone lethal.

And Charlotte saw his hand shoot out and thump the bread roll, it shattered. Then she saw him. The face among all the faces she'd ever seen, she'd perhaps looked for all her life. Still dark eyes, pale skin, small sensual mouth. He was bored. And then he saw Charlotte.

Then the doors shut and Charlotte got up. He, ahead of her was already on the platform, reaching across the newspaper stand. Charlotte jumped onto the platform, the whistle blew. Eddie spun round with the newspaper and they collided, one with the other as though moving into a longed-for embrace.

'Sorry.'

'Look, I'm really sorry.'

A final blast of the whistle. Eddie's wife tapped on the window.

'I've seen you before.' A lie. He'd seen her all his life. In that deep secret mind cellar below his thought, even his dreams.

She thought, he's not a city person. He belongs to the desert. He had a wildness and elegant control. His hand, as he pretended to adjust her balance on the impeccable always well-behaved shoes was fine as a musician's. When he'd let go of her the train had gone.

'So you've missed it too?' he kept looking into her eyes.

She liked everything about him. Too much. 'It wasn't my kind of trip after all.' And suddenly afraid, out of her depth, she turned and walked to the exit. He threw the *Herald Tribune* in a bin and followed her. She knew he was following. And her personal song started up. She created it out of the night, used bits of the city night she loved. It never let her down. And her voice was unique, thrilling as she found the first line easily, hesitating over the second.

When she had nowhere to live she always changed clothes in the lavatory of a Piccadilly hotel. The attendant, thinking she was a working girl and having nothing against those, never complained. Charlotte, wearing the exotic make-up, tight black dress split up the front, the high piled hair, was transformed. She slid the last of her money into the woman's tip bowl.

'Don't be so daft.' And the woman clawed up the coins with thick painful fingers. 'You do enough to earn this without giving it away.' And she forced Charlotte to take back the money. 'And watch the streets between here and Frith, and they've got a snoop in the lobby downstairs, so don't work that.'

At Ronnie Scott's jazz club they were coming to the end of the first set.

Charlotte served behind the bar. Among the crowd Eddie watched her, every single thing she did and her movements and actions had all the importance suddenly, as though she was on a film set. She felt she could do anything and it would be all right.

'What'll you drink? Champagne?'

Smiling, she shook her head. One small negative shake. The jazz singer caressed her last notes, and Charlotte was entranced. This was who she should be. She leaned across to the nearest musician and talked to him. She'd love the chance to sing. She didn't get it. Someone else offered her a drink. She didn't take it.

Around midnight she sat with the Soho night people at the Italian café opposite Ronnie Scott's. A female singer leaned across to Charlotte and with insultingly over-disguised malice told her she hadn't got the part in the West End musical.

Devastated, Charlotte rushed to the bar and bought a glass of white wine. She picked it up with both hands, the fix she needed. The pale yellow greenish tinged liquid, so innocent, so easing.

'I call to remembrance my song and in the night I commune with mine own heart and search out my spirits.'

She tugged her hands downwards so that the glass thumped into the bar and the wine spilled. She withdrew her hands and the glass remained alone on the counter full of little lights, inviting, poisonous. She walked out backwards, away from it.

Eddie, there on the pavement, made sure she ended the sightless walk against him. He put his arms around her lightly.

'D'you usually leave a bar backwards?' Then he noticed the beads of sweat on her face. He took a handkerchief from his pocket and dabbed her face. 'Trouble?'

'It doesn't have to be.' She was still shaking.

Eddie had enough charisma to excite the café crowd. Was he in the business? Charlotte made sure the female singer saw her leaving with him, her arm linked through his. The woman's spiteful triumph had been short-lived.

'I love your shoes,' he told Charlotte softly. 'Magic shoes. You could have adventures in those.'

He let her lead him into an unknown world. She loved the night. He understood that immediately. She made him feel alive. Again her song started up and now she had the third line, the chorus and the song was full of sensuality and passion, all the passion she could not have. Eddie was amazed by her voice.

'No, I'm not professional,' she said. 'Not trained. Not a singer. A good voice? Really? No, not married. Not with anyone.' She told him lies. She could hardly tell him the truth.

She took him to the private gambling club in Wardour Street. In the front room Soho regulars sitting on sofas made sure the pianist played Cole Porter. In the back room a poker game was in progress. The players made room for Charlotte and a glass of sparkling water was automatically placed in front of her. The players worked and lived in Soho. Waiters, cab drivers, insomniacs, a chef, a stripper, a doorman, a baker, a transvestite. The turnover at the table was quick as one after the other they left to go back to work. Eddie, amongst the waiting crowd, watched Charlotte. He found her fascinating, sultry, mercurial, untamed like a svelte jungle cat. As the night got deeper her colours became more vivid.

'You're like a forties movie star,' he told her. 'So I have seen you before.'

'Before you were you and I was I. Do you remember beloved?'

'Bells rang in your hair,' he said.

'And the blood sang in your veins,' she continued.

The players were restive. 'In or out, Charlotte?'

After six hands Charlotte got up to go back to work. Eddie asked her to eat with him. Was there somewhere still open?

'Spoilt for choice.' And she led him down to Lisle Street. They passed the bakery where the baker was just starting work. Suddenly everyone from the area was in there with bottles of champagne. It was the baker's birthday.

Eddie noticed that, although she held the glass, Charlotte didn't drink. He noticed the pale circle on her marriage finger where a ring had recently been. He noticed a lot of things. She had about her an absence – of identity, possessions. It was deliberate and necessary. He asked questions. He hadn't believed half of the things she told him earlier. He was used to not believing a lot of what he heard.

She said, 'I don't like direct questions. 'And her tone was sharp and final. She was not to be messed with.

He tried a little further. Abruptly she changed the subject.

She took him to the small Chinese restaurant, family-run, still open to the Soho regulars. The customers ate Chinese food, and the owner and his family sat at the main table and ate MacDonalds takeaways.

Eddie was keen on her. That was obvious. For a mad moment she dared to be happy. Then she realised he was married. Wasn't that his wife sitting opposite him on the train? Eddie cut through all that with a sensible plan.

'Come with me. Take the chance. I can make it work. Believe me, I can.'

She loved his eyes. They woke up every part of her that had been necessarily dead for a long time. She'd been through the married man scene badly and once again it would destroy her freedom, and this time threaten her sobriety. But she was too excited, too tempted. She rushed to the phone to speak to Terry.

'I met this man and –'

'It's wrong, Charlotte.'

'But I haven't told you anything so why d'you say it's wrong?'

'I know it's wrong, because you wake me up at three in the morning to ask me, so how can it be right?'

Then she saw Eddie speaking placatingly into a mobile phone. She knew it was to his wife. She also knew she couldn't handle the chaos of infidelity.

Back at the table he ordered a bean pancake and jasmine tea. 'Come with me as far as Milan. Then decide. D'you need to pack a bag?'

The only bag she had was on the floor beside her. It contained all her possessions. She didn't have to make the same mistakes. This didn't have to have the same ending. She longed for his first touch. She knew without doubt the pleasure he could give.

'But if you've got nothing what have you to lose?' he said.

The freedom that that nothing gives. And she saw she would lose the singing lessons but more the night. The wonderful journey from twilight to sunrise. That was a journey she trusted more than she could ever trust a person.

He was telling her how safe he'd make it, how she'd like Milan, but he knew he'd lost her. Something inside her belonged not to someone else, but some force, probably elemental.

'I know what you are,' he said. 'A traveller. And you make sure you go light.'

She went with him to Waterloo Station where he'd now take the first Eurostar to rejoin his wife in Paris. He tried to promise to see Charlotte again. He tried to give her money. 'I'm rich. I suppose that offends a free spirit like you.'

She rushed away from him into the buffet full of night workers. She talked to one of the professional beggars. She needed to buy cat food for Phil's cat. He gave her some money.

On the platform, Eddie wondered if she'd really existed.

She got a lift back to Soho to Phil's flat, changed into her street clothes, fed the cat. She even changed out of her shoes. It was almost dawn as she walked north to Regent's Park. Her song was almost complete, a song celebrating the night. The first early morning workers were setting out for the first tube. She walked along Albany Street, crossed into Primrose Hill. She climbed the steep hill and stared down at London which seemed small and innocent as the sun came up. Her song started again, suddenly stopped. But then it belonged to the night. In spite of her life and its disappointments she was all of a sudden optimistic and free.

6 a.m. and she joined the AA breakfast meeting near Camden station. She said, 'I'm Charlotte, an alcoholic. I did not take that drink.'

Originally, the small flat had the charm of a hotel suite. Easy to enter, so easy to leave. Now it has the aspect of a prison cell. Walls closing in doesn't describe it. I've got a face pack on, an eye gel cools my eyes and I'm painting my toenails scarlet. When all of these things dry I'll do my singing exercises. Yes, I remember the early days in this flat. Commitments? The minimum. And everything was new and stylish and glamorous and none of it mine.

A horrible moment in the mirror just now. Was it grey I saw on the side of my hair? It could have been the light. It had better be the light. My hair has never let me down. It's ageless. I've got the shoes from the top of the clothes cupboard. Italian tender leather shoes, with an art deco design in pink and gold, and elegant skyscraper heels. Wonderful shoes like no others that I actually enjoy looking at. That's about all I can do with them. I can squeeze into them – just – for the singing. They massacre my toes. I have to return my poor pinched feet into the easeful wide-toed trainers. Let's face it, my feet can't take it. I'm too heavy and my ankles are swollen.

But I'm going to slim down and exercise and any minute I'll be able to go out in these shoes.

The singing teacher squeezes me into his West End classes tighter than my feet fit into these shoes. If I'm five minutes late he starts on about his high-class problems and we lose track altogether. My French isn't his idea of French, but I have to sing in the Bal Musette dancehalls in the Pyrenees and sing so they understand. My audience is mainly the curists taking the water in the spas and they like to come and dance in the afternoons. They like a good time. I'll say that for them. The singing teachers put the new exercises on tape. I can't possibly reach that high D. Does he think I'm Maria Callas? I can't reach it also because the neighbours wouldn't like it. But I squeeze some sound up into my head as the shoes, in turn, squeeze my toes.

I've read the latest letters from my ex-husband going on about my faults. He seems to know them better than I do. Another letter from the bank. I won't open that. Two from the community charge. A brown one, I'm definitely not going to touch. I've got my Eurostar ticket ready with passport, credit cards, medical insurance, French francs. I keep thinking there's some vital support document I've forgotten. Thank God I'm off. The homeopathic chemist wants his bill paid up front before he sends the medicine. He says I never pay my bills. My accountant says the same. He says I was mad to lose that husband. They've all got plenty to say. They know me. I'm too known, too predictable. I wish I could just walk out of this door and be free, each moment a new start. But they don't know about the singing. That's my secret. My real ID.

I'll either get a black cab at the top of the street or call the minicab service to Waterloo. But first I have to go to the AA meeting around the corner. My trouble – I'm inclined to leave my addiction behind on Waterloo Station. I'm as free as a bird when I leave England. Freer still on arrival in Paris. Free with the drinks all right. But then comes the morning after and there's nothing free about that. No, my mornings after start the night before. The shakes, the jumping heart, the unbearable restlessness in my legs, the cramps, the lot. I can't bear being in my body to tell the truth. No sleep. Not remotely. I won't think about that now. Just sing. He's given me a new song. 'Around Midnight'. Because I told him I love songs about the night. Things always get better when it's dark.

I hope Terry's at the AA meeting. I need to talk with him about not picking up that first drink. If you don't take the first one you can't get drunk. I always thought the fourth was the problem.

I don't look my age. I haven't lost my looks. And my drinking isn't really the problem. And it's modest, considering what I hear in the rooms. I even wonder if I am an alky. I could be dramatising it all. I heard that the woman opposite reckons I'm overdramatic. They've really got me pinned down in this neighbourhood. Can't hide a thing. Look, I can give up. Haven't I proved it? I'm sixty days without a drink. Terry says anyone can get off drink. It's staying off that's the problem. He also says alcoholism is the only disease that tells you you haven't got a disease.

I think I'll bin the post. It's all demanding, really exhausting. And the phone's ringing again. Never stops. I'm too visible and that's the truth. I've considered changing my name. Sometimes I long for escape. To escape into the night. To be swallowed up into the city night and be remade.

Terry wants me to be sociable at the meetings. Talk to other members. Fit in. I've never fitted in in my life. But I love singing. I still love that. I could have had a career.

That story about Charlotte, by the way, I made it up. I lied about all that. That's how I'd like it to be.

The real story

The real story is this: I'm supposed to go to my singing lesson but I'm laid out in bed with a colossal hangover. Another lost day. Curtains closed, swallowing Coke. I told the singing teacher I had flu. He said, 'Again? You're the sickest person I've known outside of a hospital.' He doesn't believe me. No one has flu that often. But I think he'll keep me on because I do have something. A certain thrill in my voice. I was born with that.

One ankle is swollen because I fell out of my shoes during some blacked out moment in that mad, bad evening. Even with the anaesthetic effects of all that drink I could still feel some pain as the ankle twisted. No idea how I got home. I don't want to know. I know singing is the only way that I'll get over this drinking thing. Singing out the pain. I don't have a drink problem. My problem is I'm sixty in a minute and drink makes me forget it. I'll take another trank and two pain killers. In fact I'll get back on pills. Drink is a bad deal.

I'd like to ring Terry at AA but he's dropped me too. Says he can't handle my disease. It's bigger than both of us. I should consider going in. Terry said it less elegantly than that. And I thought AA was supposed to help drinkers, not throw them out. I mean if I could give up I wouldn't go to AA. I can always top anxiety with a worse thought. That never lets me down. I've just realised I'm absolutely on my own. Who comes round? Who could I ring to come round? If I died in here who would find me? I've suddenly got old age fears and nowhere to be with them. Could I get it together for another marriage?

Fate is another dropped friend. I always thought I'd marry a Hollywood guy and live in L.A. and here I am wondering which old age people's home to check into.

When the remorse settles and the crawling in my veins stops – God, I hope I don't get a stroke. That's what they warned me about the last time when the doctor was called. My blood pressure goes right up after that kind of drinking. That's when you get a stroke and the doctor said if you're really unlucky you *don't* die. I've got myself really frightened. I've promised God if He gets me out of this I'll never do it again. As soon as I can get up I'll drink a lot of water, wash my face, put an iced bandage on my foot. The cramp in my calf again. Like a dog biting. The trouble is I romanticised AA. I've got to blame something.

That story about the Eurostar trip and the singing job in the Pyrenees, all lies. Why do I lie? Face packs, glamour, travel, escape and youth. I suppose I lie because that's what I'd like. I long for the night to come and heal everything. With the night I'm in with a chance.

The truth behind the real story

Now I'm telling the truth. I started out for the singing lesson but was far too rocky. I got to Victoria Station and the crowd huffed and puffed around me. Commuters sped towards me, arrows of hostility. I felt I was in the middle of a war. Yes, they came at me from every angle, not unlike one of those space invader games and I thought I'll have to have a drink. What else can I do. It's better than a crack up and crack up comes next.

I'm nineteen days sober and too raw for this scene. I bought a return ticket for Balham. The teacher could only fit me in at his home and he lives on the edge of the railway line. Then I phoned Terry. Wiping the sweat off my face I said nineteen days might be as far as I got. He was calm. He told me to get a cab to the nearest AA meeting.

So I got in a cab and stopped to buy a bottle of mineral water. I told the driver to find a quick way to the central London church meeting in the crypt. Then I changed my mind. I'd had enough suddenly. I couldn't anymore handle the handling of the drink. I told the driver to go to the rehab clinic. The private one with the soothing shrinks.

'But that's in Richmond,' he said.

I'd done enough geographical escapes in my life. What was so far away about Richmond? I've got the music sheets in my bag with the shoes. The lovely pink art deco shoes with the skyscraper heels. They're like old friends. What adventures I've had in them. I can't get them on anymore.

I see myself as a map, half the territory stained with addiction. The rest? Under doubt. The strong patch, where the music is. No addiction there. And so it goes. Drink, don't drink, drink. Both states no good. And the colours on the map become stronger and spread as the addiction again takes over.

'Stop at the next pub. I'll get out there.'

Of course I wouldn't go in, to a clinic. That is a failure beyond what I can contain. I'll go to the singing lesson. I'll just have a drink first. That story I told about the hangover behind closed curtains. I left a lot out. Of course it's not the truth.

I long for the night. With the night I'm in with a chance.

My story

They gave me another shot just now. I wanted to clean my face then realised I hadn't got any things. Yes, I've got the shoes. I saw them when I slowly turned onto my right side. Elegantly together on the floor, pink and gold and absolutely beautiful. For some reason a song I wrote keeps coming into my mind. It's made up of bits of night in the city. I wrote it years ago.

The doctor prodded my stomach. Not too good. How long had it been like that? I didn't care to remember. Then the nurse came up and said she'd put my things in the ward locker, I didn't have any things. It seems I just brought my shoes. She slammed shut my ward locker and asked how I'd clean my teeth. I said Terry would bring me what I needed. If I could just get the zap to ring him. Things? I always had things. Too many of them.

Then it occurred to me I'd feel a lot better if I could get out of here. Wait for the night, then go. I'd like to go to Ronnie Scott's. Get in for the first set and have a club sandwich and Coca Cola these days. I love Ronnie Scott's. But I can't go to places on my own.

The student nurse noticed my shoes. 'Oh, they are beautiful.' And she picked one up and the heel, it flopped down and swung, broken. I wanted to cry. How had that happened? Seeing my face she understood. 'It can be mended easily.' She was reassuring. 'They just stick it back on.'

I wished I could be mended as easily. I knew it was bad news when the winter afternoon darkened, and as always when that happened, I felt more cheerful and I tried to sit up, get up, go. I couldn't lift my head. Yes, I knew it might be all up with me, even before the doctor put the sign on my bed: 'Nil by mouth'.

'We'll get you ready for surgery.'

So I escaped in another way. In my mind. Thought took me away.

Why did I invent Charlotte? She's not a lie. She's who I should have been. I knew Soho in the old days. It was full of bohemians then. I was so in awe of them. How I wished I was one of those Soho regulars right in the centre of the existentialist group, black drainpipe trousers, Jean Paul Sartre, trad jazz, the night boat to Paris. How I wished I was free like that. I always had too much luggage. I was too known. Fame had come too early and easily. I was spoiled. I couldn't go anywhere unnoticed. And my husband – he smothered me with luxury until I could hardly breathe. That's why I told that story about Charlotte. I'd have loved to be her. I've always liked stations. But in those early days with the success, it was taxis and chauffeur-driven cars. And my husband – always there. Yet stations for me summed up what I wanted and could never have – escape.

And the story behind Charlotte. I made her struggle and strive. How I longed for that. To have to try. To rise up from the anonymity into a talented and deserved recognition. To do the unusual. Sing in a Bal

Musette bar in the Pyrenees. She had obstacles that made the fulfilment exciting. That's what I should have had.

And the one behind her. In the light of what I'm going through now – not so bad. Curtains drawn on a sickly hangover. Well, I always put a good face on things.

And the last one. I should have shared her at the AA meetings and saved my life. But I always had to put forward the best image. That's who I am. Optimistic. It may have cost me my life.

I've had so much smothering. I loved the idea of not knowing what came next. I loved the idea of really working for the singing so it became valuable.

Eddie? I did know an Eddie once. That's not a lie. He was sitting in the dining-car of a train going to Nice. He looked at me, that special look, deep, very personal. He looked again and saw even more. We were meant to know each other. I've never forgotten the unexpectedness of it. I wonder now what would have happened if I'd just walked across and joined him.

But I was in the gilded cage. Singing, yes, but it was still a cage. My husband was so tuned in to my every need he anticipated it before I even had it. I would say my life was full of sugar. Sugary and soft and without edges. How I needed to be lean and spiritually muscled to reach for what I wanted. No wonder I started to drink.

The stories are layers of me I should have had. Only the shoes are the same. It's strange I made up these women, but if I concentrate enough on them maybe God will forgive me.

I heard the head nurse say, 'She used to be a singer. Really well known. You won't remember her. Before your time.'

They asked who I wanted to see. I thought about Terry. Then my singing teacher. Then they said my husband was here. Of course he'd find me.

The chauffeur brought in the flowers, fruit, mineral water and case of nightdresses. My husband said he'd move me to a private room. He tried to hold my hand. I'd never seen him look so old. I kept looking at the shoes. If I could just get the will to sit up, stand up and escape. But the shoes – of course they can't be worn. Both of us, broken.

The doctor pulled the screens around, then spoke candidly, all of it bad news. I could feel my husband's tears splash onto my hand.

And I went back to Charlotte and the song I'd made up. When I sing that song nothing bad can happen to me.

I told them if it comes to it to bury me in my shoes.

24. Terry

by

Terry

From fifteen to forty-six I used drink and drugs on a daily basis which led to police cells, hospitals, mental hospitals, and prison. At forty-six I came into AA. I've got thirteen years free of addiction. I feel peace beyond that which I knew existed.

I'm not a victim of my past, my childhood, my upbringing. I'm not a victim to addiction, and the discovery I made was that the only problem I had in life was fear. I'll lose what I've got and won't get what I want. I don't have that fear in my life now. I have found a power greater than me and everyday life is fantastic. Today I love everyone, myself included.

Nobody can take anything away from me. You can give to me but you can't take anything from me. Today I walk in the sunlight of the spirit. There are no down days. Every time I wake up it's a blank page and I write the script. All I've got is now. I live in the present, happy, joyous and free. It's there for everyone. I'm not special or different. I can look around me and see the beauty in things I never noticed. I've got this serenity inside me, so whatever happens on the outside doesn't matter.

I'm free.